From Behind the Desk to the Front of the Stage

From Behind the Desk to the Front of the Stage

How to Enhance Your Presentation Skills

David Worsfold

BEP BUSINESS EXPERT PRESS

From Behind the Desk to the Front of the Stage: How to Enhance Your Presentation Skills

First published in 2019 by
Business Expert Press, LLC
222 East 46th Street, New York, NY 10017
www.businessexpertpress.com

ISBN-13: 978-1-63157-909-7 (paperback)
ISBN-13: 978-1-63157-910-3 (e-book)

Business Expert Press Human Resource Management and Organizational Behavior Collection

Collection ISSN: 1946-5637 (print)
Collection ISSN: 1946-5645 (electronic)

Cover and interior design by Exeter Premedia Services Private Ltd., Chennai, India

First edition: 2019

10 9 8 7 6 5 4 3 2 1

Printed in the United States of America.

Abstract

A practical guide to presentation skills based on four decades of experience of public speaking around the world and of training and coaching people.

It deals with all aspects of public speaking, but with a particular emphasis on the skills people need to be successful in their business career or when representing or presenting to a wide range of organizations.

It covers a wide range of different presentation skills, including making an impact in the boardroom, conference speaking, using multimedia, and bringing complex subjects to life, as well as hosting everything from roundtables to awards presentations.

There are many practical hints and tips and exercises that people can do to improve their presentation style, as well as detailed advice on how to create and structure content to make maximum impact.

It has a business focus and is aimed at people who need to be good on their feet in order to progress in their careers or promote the topics they are interested in. It also covers some of the challenging events such as awards ceremonies, as well as formal and informal social occasions.

Its USPs are that it takes people on their journey from behind their desk to the front of the stage in a sympathetic and insightful way, helping them to build on their strengths and gain confidence as they go along.

Keywords

audiences; autocues; awards ceremonies; conferences; content; cue cards; facilitating; gestures; humor; interactive technology; introductions; microphones; pitch and pace; powerpoint; preparation; presentations; public speaking; relaxation techniques; rhetoric; roundtables; scripts; slides; stance; structure; style; video; visualization; voice; voice exercises

Contents

Introduction

A speech is a solemn responsibility. The man who makes a bad 30-minute speech to 200 people wastes only half an hour of his own time. But he wastes one hundred hours of the audience's time—more than four days—which should be a hanging offence.
—Jenkin Lloyd Jones, Unitarian minister and uncle of architect
Frank Lloyd Wright

There comes a time in the careers of everyone who wants to be successful and reach the top of their chosen profession when they have to start standing up in front of audiences and—here is the tough bit—speaking to them.

For some, this is a challenge they relish and seem to rise to with ease. For many, however, this journey from behind the desk to the front of the stage is filled with terror. Surveys of popular opinion on what people most fear in life frequently put public speaking at the top—it even comes out ahead of death in some polls.[1] That is a sobering thought for anyone grappling with the prospect of having to stand up in front of colleagues, business prospects, conference audiences, or even family and friends.

Why is this? And, more importantly, what can people do to overcome that fear and master the art of effective public speaking?

Running away is one option. In modern business life, however, that will be career limiting. Despite the explosion in digital communication channels and social media, people still place a very high value on face-to-face communication. People relate to people more than screens and machines. We want to hear stories told by people. We want to look people in the eye to judge the truth and sincerity of what they are saying. Often, we want our emotions to be engaged: we want to be inspired, moved,

---

[1] "Are You Scared of Public Speaking?" 2013. *The Guardian.* https://theguardian.com/commentisfree/poll/2013/oct/30/public-speaking-phobias-scared-glossophobia (accessed July 9, 2018).

entertained, enthused, and enriched. In this world dominated by screens, working at home (alone), and social media, the value of good face-to-face communication has soared.

That makes the prospect of stepping out from behind a desk and striding toward the front of the stage even more daunting. It also explains why that journey is so important, and why we must all be brave enough to navigate its many potential hazards.

Most people faced with the prospect of having to start that journey and speak to an audience will instantly find that fear and nerves take a tight hold.

Let them take over and you will struggle on all sorts of levels, letting yourself and your audience down. Nobody can take away the nerves. Indeed, they should not really try to because you will need that nervous energy to help you project your content and your personality to the audience. Anyone who promises to *cure* your nerves is guilty of selling a false promise. The trick is to harness the nervous energy and channel it in positive directions. It can help you do a better job than you might ever have imagined yourself capable of.

I have trained many people in public speaking and have never once promised to take away those nervous butterflies, but I do endeavor to get them flying in formation by the end of a course.

The advice and techniques I coach on my courses have stood the test of time and earned the appreciation of many novice speakers, as I have taken them on that journey from behind the desk to the front of the stage. They have also helped experienced speakers, including chief executives and business leaders, take their presentational style to a fresh, more engaging level.

The one thing I will never do is turn people into a boring clone of the safe but oh-so-dull management consultant. We have all heard them at conferences, armed with their endless slides, measured speaking style, perfectly constructed presentations (superficially at least), but devoid of personality. Few remember them, or more importantly, what they said.

The best, most engaging speakers build on their own personal strengths to communicate their message to their listeners in a way that will make it memorable. That is the constant focus of the advice in this book.

I am very grateful to two very experienced speakers and trainers for the advice, guidance, and comments that have made this book better than it otherwise would have been. Stuart McLean, who has had a long career as a human resources director in the publishing industry and Caryl Oliver, trainer, consultant, and international sportswoman. While their advice has improved the book, its defects are still mine.

CHAPTER 1

You Want to Succeed and So Does Your Audience!

They can because they think they can.

—Virgil, ancient Roman poet

Whether you think you can or whether you think you can't—you are right.

—Henry Ford, founder of the Ford Motor Company

There are people who are imbued with supreme self-confidence who will leap at the opportunity to stand up in front of colleagues, clients, conference audiences, or dinner guests and make a speech. It will not necessarily be a good speech because that takes time, effort, planning, and practice. But, they have that first crucial ingredient required for that journey to the front of the stage—self-belief.

If you are one of the vast majority for whom that degree of self-belief does not come easily, you have to find it from somewhere. This does not mean striving for a false persona that will probably just appear brash and pushy to most people, but instead laying a firm foundation using your own personality and its many strengths, which may be hidden from you or seem rather elusive when faced with the challenge of making a speech in public.

This means starting by striking out some of the obvious negative thoughts that can grip you before you even get to the stage.

People's fear of public speaking often starts with the thought of dozens—if not hundreds—of pairs of eyes staring at them, scrutinizing their every word and action. This fear is almost always misplaced. Is that focus on critical scrutiny your mindset when you sit in an audience? It is very unlikely that it is so; learn to treat audiences as supportive, wanting you to be successful, and effective in getting your message across to them.

You want to succeed and your audience wants you to succeed, so be positive from the moment you accept a speaking engagement, whether that be opening a conference, making a major sales pitch, delivering a detailed discourse on a complex subject, explaining a change in the way a business runs, or even speaking at a wedding reception.

If you think about what works for you when you are in an audience and what does not, then you will be well on the way to understanding how to make a good speech or presentation.

If you are not experienced, do not start by thinking you would like to come across as the most inspirational speaker you have ever heard. Start with more modest ambitions. Focus on what you know does not work, such as speaking too quietly, using a monotone voice, over-complicated slides, too much statistical information, or awful jokes. Now, ask yourself how you are going to avoid those obvious pitfalls.

Keeping it simple is a core mantra for effective public speaking, never more so than when you are a relative novice. Do not try to be clever if you are not certain you can pull it off. The clever techniques you have seen employed by speakers who you admire have almost certainly been polished up through years of practice. They will have learned what works for them and their audiences. They will have tried a variety of techniques to find out what is most effective for them. This perseverance is what has made them successful, although they will almost certainly have experienced some failures along the way. They made sure they learned from them, moved on, and did a better job next time. It is rather like the top-class golfer who misses an easy putt: by the time they hit the tee shot on the next hole, they have put that behind them. They do not dwell on it because they know that will pull them down. That is how we must learn to cope with the occasional bad experience with a presentation: learn from it, but put it firmly behind us.

There are very few circumstances in which an audience, or part of it, wants a speaker to fail.

The most obvious are hostile political audiences. They are tough—very tough—which is why even the most experienced politicians are nowadays kept away from them. Political spin doctors do not want their charges thrown off their stride by well-timed, pointed interventions, or hecklers. For them, it is all about control. That is something perhaps many other speakers can learn too, as the more you feel in control, the better job you will do.

Hostile audiences in the world of business and commerce are very rare, so are not worth losing sleep over.

You will almost certainly be speaking to audiences that want you to do your best. At any event, the majority of the audience would rather be where they are than where you are and are not there to judge you harshly. You can take great comfort from this.

They actually want you to succeed. Whatever role you are there to play, they want you to do it well, so the event meets their expectations. Nobody wants to come away from a conference thinking all the speakers were boring or had nothing new to say, or find themselves cringing at the leaden after-dinner speaker with a grim repertoire of poorly told jokes.

For a business presentation, people want to be engaged and informed. Those are their core expectations, and they are not as hard to meet as people might imagine.

The audience will be on your side when you stand up. The trick is to keep them with you.

One thing for certain you will never know whether you can do that if you run away from opportunities to speak or make a presentation. Of course, the early opportunities must be the right ones. They must be situations in which you can—once you have banished the more corrosive negative thoughts—imagine yourself succeeding in if you get the right advice and support. This book is firmly focused on the sort of practical advice that can get you up and running.

Getting Started

- Believe in yourself.
- Remember that audiences want you to succeed.
- Start with simple techniques and structures.
- Do not be too clever.
- Do not let nerves drag you down: harness them to create positive energy.

CHAPTER 2

Preparation: The Foundation of Success

The human brain starts working the moment you are born and never stops working until you stand up to speak in public.
—Sir George Jessel, 19th century British judge

We have probably all seen people freeze when they stand up to speak to an audience. Nerves, fear of failure, and simple panic overwhelm them. No one feels comfortable, least of all the person on their feet who sees their career, reputation, and prospects draining away before their very eyes.

How can we ensure that does not happen to us? One of the keys is preparation, preparation, and more preparation. Never underestimate the value of proper preparation when it comes to public speaking. Even what can appear to be the most spontaneous of events or presentations is often carefully rehearsed and runs within a meticulously prepared framework.

Shortcuts in preparation usually only have one destination—failure. It might not be total failure, but it will be a speech that falls well short of your expectations and the expectations of your audience. Cutting corners on preparation when you are making a presentation is a fast track to disaster, or at the very least, frayed nerves, sleepless nights, and that corrosive panic.

Some inexperienced speakers are deceived by the ease with which an experienced speaker makes a presentation into thinking that it is easy. It is not. In general, the more you prepare and the more you polish it up beforehand, the more your presentation will shine.

This focus on preparation is about putting you in control of a stressful situation as much as is possible. It is about not leaving things to chance or taking too casual an "It will be alright on the night" approach to an event. Making lists of all the things you need to know in advance and can get control of is a very good habit to get into as it greatly reduces the chances of something unexpected fraying your nerves on the day.

Preparation can be broken down into five key areas:

The Five Points of Proper Preparation

1. Know your subject

If you are making a major presentation, it goes without saying that you must know your subject. The better you know your subject, the more confident you are going to be standing up and talking about it. This will come across to an audience and will build their rapport with you. Mark Twain once wrote "Tell the truth and you will have nothing to remember." What he meant was that the better you know your subject and believe in what you are saying, the easier you will find it to communicate that to other people.

Often, you will be given a brief by your boss or a conference organizer. This is clearly helpful, but if you feel it is taking you too far outside of your knowledge and expertise, then raise that well in advance of the presentation so that, if possible, the brief can be revised. If not, then you might find yourself having to do a lot of additional research, in which case allow yourself plenty of time for that.

Even a short speech opening a conference requires you to have a clear grasp of the issues, agenda, speakers, and topics they are covering. It may also involve dealing with some of the event logistics such as where breakout sessions take place and who the sponsors are. These details are important to the audience and probably to the smooth running and commercial success of the event as well, so make sure you master them.

2. Know your audience

Who is in the audience? Why are they there? What level of seniority are they? What are the key issues from their perspective? How many will be there?

The key challenge with many business or similar presentations is judging the prior knowledge of an audience and the key issues they expect you to address. Making a properly informed judgment about where the balance lies is critical to the success of a presentation. If you start-off a presentation at too basic a level, telling people things they already know, they will quickly switch off. At the other end of the spectrum, if you assume too much knowledge and pitch it beyond an audience, you will again be in danger of losing their interest very quickly.

When it comes to the size of an audience, remember that event organizers often talk up numbers, so do not set your heart on a certain number turning up to hear you as you may be disappointed (or relieved) when you arrive. It is important to have an approximate idea of the size of the audience because that will help you with your preparation, especially if you decide to use some of the visualization techniques discussed later.

If you have been given an inflated expectation of audience numbers and they fall well short of that on the day, do not let your disappointment show to those who are there. They deserve your very best as they have made the effort to come and listen to you. It is about the people who are there, not the ones who are not (or were never going to be).

3. **Know your venue**

You want to feel as comfortable as possible in a stressful situation, and knowing the venue, its size, and its layout certainly helps. If you can visit it beforehand, then do so, although this is a rare luxury. If it is going to have a purpose-built stage with lectern, screen, seats, and so on, ask for a visual of the platform and arrive early on the day to check it out. Also, put on your list to check in advance to ask whether there will be a photographer and whether there is a video relay onto a large screen.

Unexpected flash photography can be distracting, so try to get an idea of where the photographer will be taking pictures from. Pictures of events have a lot of value to the organizers, so be as co-operative as possible.

Many large events have a live video relay to big screens on the stage behind you, and one of the most disconcerting traps for the unwary is suddenly being confronted with a huge close-up of yourself speaking. Try not to be taken by surprise. If possible, ask to see what you will look like on the screen during the rehearsal, so you are prepared for the shock.

I was once giving a welcome speech during an awards ceremony at the Royal Albert Hall in London. I was using a lapel mic (see Chapter 7 on microphones) and walking around the front of the stage. I had rehearsed the speech two or three times earlier in the day and was quite comfortable with everything. However, there was a live video relay onto two huge screens mounted either side of the massive pipe organ that dominated the back of the stage in the Royal Albert Hall. These screens were still being set up when I rehearsed so I did not see them in action until I was live on stage in front of nearly 2,000 people. There was a moment when I turned sideways to speak to one side of the hall and caught a glimpse of myself. It was a shock and nearly put me off. I took a deep breath, carried on, and made sure I did not glance behind me again.

Ever since then, I have been careful to check how I will look on screen and to keep it firmly behind me (see Figure 2.1).

Figure 2.1 The author keeping the big screen image of himself firmly behind him

Source: Credit: Infopro Digital

4. Know your technology

Make sure you know what technology is involved or available and whether it is expected that you will use it. This covers sound, lighting, and visual aids, including PowerPoint presentations. When you get to the venue, ask to see the rostrum, controls for slides, lighting level when you will be speaking, and do a sound check. Find out whether you actually control the slides or are just sending a signal to a production desk and ask what to do and which buttons to press if you need to go back to an earlier slide. It is remarkably easy when you are nervous and agitated on stage to press a control button too hard or too many times and jump several slides ahead of yourself. Make sure you know how to go back.

At any major event using microphones, you will routinely be asked to do a sound check before your presentation and may even have an opportunity to do a *top and tail* rehearsal of the beginning and end of your speech. However, this usually takes place without the stage lighting fully on. Ask to see it, so you know how bright it is going to be and where the main spotlights are mounted. You do not want to find yourself suddenly dazzled and blinking at the start of your presentation or squinting because the lights are poorly directed and you cannot escape the harsh glare.

Speakers need to be well lit when they are on stage, so you must expect the lighting to be bright. However, it should not be so bright or directly in your eyes that it is distracting. If you are not comfortable with it, when you see it at the rehearsal, speak to the organizers and see whether anything can be done to alleviate the problem.

If you are going to be moving around the stage during your presentation, you also need to be aware of how much of the stage is well lit and where any dark patches might be. Actors are trained to *find the light*, so they are always well lit when on stage and professional presenters do the same. If you step into a partial shadow, it is a subconscious visual cue for the audience to dis-engage from the presentation.

It is also important to check that any multimedia material incorporated in your presentation plays properly, especially if you are running video clips (how to use multimedia content effectively is dealt with in Chapter 10). Never take someone else's promise that it works for granted: try it yourself.

5. Rehearsal

Practice your speech. If appropriate, write out a full text (we will look at the advantages and disadvantages of this in Chapter 9). Ask a friend or colleague to listen to it. Make sure it is the right length by timing yourself. If you think it might be too long, cut it. When you rehearse, you should stand and imagine yourself in the room or hall where you will be speaking. You also need to rehearse your body language and gestures as well, regardless of how self-conscious you might feel when doing so. Some people find all of these things easier to do in front of a mirror or even to video themselves rehearsing part or all of a presentation, which is easy to do nowadays.

If you do rehearse in front of a friend or colleague, invite feedback and be prepared to act on their constructive suggestions.

You need to feel as comfortable as possible on the day, leaving little to chance. Ask the conference organizers whether you can rehearse on the platform before the audience arrives, even if it is only the start and finish of your presentation. Ask where you will be sitting, when you are expected to go to the rostrum, and what you should do when you have finished, especially if there is a question and answer session to follow your speech. If you are not happy with these arrangements, say so and get them changed if possible.

A good conference organizer should tell you all this. You do need to know these things so that you are not sitting there worrying unnecessarily. You may have done everything possible to relax, you may be confident with the content of your presentation and have got those nerves under control. All of that good work can be undone in an instant if you suddenly panic about when you should go up to the stage because you forgot to check.

Ask how you will be introduced. Will the chair just announce you or will they read out a lot of biographical detail? Check which points they are going to highlight just in case you have built any of them into the introduction of your speech. Often, a good event facilitator will pick out something that illustrates your authority to speak on a topic; you may have expected to do this yourself, so you do not want to be repeating what has just been said.

The introduction may be over the PA system, often referred to by event producers as the *voice of god*. At smaller events, it could be the complete opposite with you expected to introduce yourself, which you will have to think carefully about how to do effectively. It is all about not being caught unawares.

Finally, check your route to the rostrum. Look out for steps, cables, projectors, and lights as there can be few worse preludes to a speech than tripping up before you even start. You might want to practice your walk to the stage if it involves negotiating several steps so that you can feel confident; you will be looking good from the moment the audience's eyes fall on you. Some stages have high steps and a lot of uplighting at the floor level. Again, if you are worried that something might present a hazard, say so.

If you are speaking from a rostrum, check that it is a good height for you. If you are especially tall or particularly short, you should talk to the organizers in advance so that they can make appropriate adjustments (see Figure 2.2).

Even if you are the first speaker in a session, never leave your script or cue cards on the rostrum—keep them with you at all times. Another speaker may rehearse after you and accidently pick up your papers or a diligent production assistant may think they are left over from a previous presentation and clear them away.

Figure 2.2 **Check your route to the rostrum: Look out for steps, cables, and lights**

Source: Credit: Infopro Digital

Benjamin Franklin's oft-quoted adage "Fail to Prepare: Prepare to Fail" is rarely more pertinent than when it comes to public speaking. Do not cut corners and never let self-confidence get the better of you.

Venue Checklist

- Sound—do a sound check.
- Lighting—ask to see the stage lighting as it will be when you are speaking.
- AV controls—make sure you understand them.
- Photography—be prepared for flash photography.
- Seating arrangements—find out where you should sit before and after your presentation.
- Check how you will be introduced.
- Always plot and check your route to the rostrum.

CHAPTER 3

Learning to Relax

I do some form of breathing exercises during a pressure situation. It definitely helps. Every time, before I hit a key shot, I take a deep breath and cleanse the mind.

—Paul Azinger, American golfer

Nerves are inevitable: they are part and parcel of giving a live performance. There is very little we can do to stop the butterflies: there is a lot we can do to get them flying in formation to help us do a great job. What we must aim to do is to harness that nervous energy and turn it from a negative into a positive force to help you project yourself and your message more effectively when you are up on that stage.

You will naturally be nervous before a speech, but do not run away from those nerves. The best performers harness their nerves and use the energy they generate to enhance their presence on the stage. They also usually have routines that help them relax and focus on the task in hand. It is a question of striking a sensible balance between taking the destructive edge off your nerves by learning to relax, but also retaining and channeling some of that nervous energy to help energize and lift your performance.

Practice and preparation are the best defenses against being overwhelmed by nerves as the moment you get to your feet approaches. In the previous chapter, the emphasis was on using your preparation to give you a genuine sense of control over the public speaking experience. Getting that right means taking away a lot of the unnecessary stress that can set nerves running amok and ruin your chances of giving a good account of yourself on stage.

You need to minimize the number of things to worry about in those vital moments before starting a presentation. Make sure your notes or script are in good order and in your hands. Be clear on when you take to the stage, where you stand, how you control the AV, and where you go at the end. All these little things can suddenly loom large if not taken care of beforehand and destroy the most determined attempts to channel that nervous energy.

People often worry that others will see that they are nervous. They should not worry, as most people in any audience will understand that nerves are part of the challenge of public speaking.

Often, they will not even be aware of your nerves as most signs of the usual level of nervousness are almost invisible to other people. You may be very aware of them, but the audience does not see them.

Nobody can see your heart beating faster or detect that you might be breathing a little faster and more deeply than usual.

Up to a point, nobody will see the slight tremor in your hands, although if this is how your nerves manifest themselves, you should be wary of holding large sheets of loose paper when you are on stage. By the time the small shaking of your hand has traveled the length of a piece of paper, it could be visible. If you do find your hands shake a little when you are nervous, then you should avoid holding loose, flimsy sheets of paper. Use card instead or a clipboard, or make sure you have a lectern to put your papers on.

One of the more common signs of nerves that could be visible is feeling flushed. We usually feel it rather more than other people can see its effects. This response usually stops around the neck, so if you are aware of it and sufficiently conscious of it that it adds to your stress and nerves, then wear a shirt or blouse that has a sufficiently high neck or buttons up to cover it. Before you start worrying about it too much, ask friends and colleagues whether they notice you looking flushed. Often, it is the case that we are far more aware of these things ourselves and others only notice when their attention is drawn to it.

Nerves can have a debilitating effect on performance if you let them get control. All top performers, whether presenters, actors, or singers, have exercises they do to help them relax. These focus especially on breathing and reducing tension in the facial, neck, and shoulder muscles.

Why Is This Important?

If we allow too much tension to creep into our body, then our voice is affected. This will mean it will speed up or get higher in pitch, often sounding thin and less authoritative as a result. Controlling pace and pitch is very important, and there is plenty more on why that is so in Chapter 6. Relaxing, breathing, and reducing muscle tension make an important contribution to making the most of your voice and help to look after it.

There are tried and tested techniques you can use on the big day, and every speaker should develop a routine that works for them. This will require you to make some time and space for yourself before going on the stage. This is worth doing, but is frequently a lot easier said than done, as you will often have many other things distracting you. Often, inexperienced speakers welcome these distractions as they will take their mind off the daunting challenge they are about to undertake. This is not the best approach. You need to make some time for yourself.

Theater, television studios, and some large performance and conference venues have dressing rooms or green rooms (green is thought to be the most relaxing color) where performers can sit and prepare beforehand. If those are available, then use them. Most venues where business presentations are made will not have such facilities, so you will have to find a space where you can go through your simple pre-stage routine. Try to find somewhere where you can do this. Sometimes, this means dropping out of the pre-conference or pre-awards hurly-burly of exhibitions and receptions even if people are demanding your presence. Do not be afraid to excuse yourself from this: you are the one going on the stage, others are not.

As speakers gain experience, they quickly become much less self-conscious about their pre-performance relaxation routine, as they realize what an important contribution it makes to the quality of their performance.

There is no one routine that works for everybody. There are, however, some elements that could be included and which every speaker should try until they find a routine that is effective.

Breath Control

Filling your lungs with air and expanding your diaphragm is going to make a significant difference to the quality of your voice and your ability to project it, especially in a large venue.

Often, this involves just standing quietly beforehand, taking long, deep breaths. Learn to take in a very deep breath; let it out slowly. Try it two or three times, making the exhalation last longer each time. Preferably, you should be standing, although these exercises can be done sitting down if you are well-positioned in the chair and sitting up straight. You can vary this exercise by humming at different pitches or hissing as you let your breath out.

Reduce Muscle Tension

You can use simple facial and neck exercises to relax your jaw and mouth. Rotating your jaw a few times in both directions will create more flexibility around your mouth. Open your mouth as wide as you can a few times. If you tend to tense up around the neck, then leaning your head slowly from side-to-side toward your shoulders will help. Rotating shoulders also helps reduce the tension in and around the neck.

For some people, the problem is clenching their fists when they are on stage which sends tension all the way up the arms and into the shoulders. If this is your problem, try spreading your fingers wide and stretching your arms out in front of you and then slowly drawing your arms back bringing your hands together behind your back. These exercises should be repeated two or three times to ensure you get the full benefit from them.

Clenching hands tight is a common manifestation of nerves, and it is the one that can be taken onto the stage. If there is a lectern, there is sometimes a temptation to grab hold of the sides. This can result in you gripping it very tightly, sending that tension straight up your arms, through the shoulders, and into the neck. It can also make you look very wooden and static to the audience. By all means, rest your hands on the rostrum from time-to-time, but be careful not to grab hold of it as if it is about to develop a life of its own and run off.

Voice

It is not always very easy to exercise the voice before a business presentation, and in most situations, probably not essential. The bigger the event, the more challenging the venue, or the longer the presentation, then the more advisable it is to incorporate a few gentle exercises just to wake up your vocal chords and clear your throat properly. Simple humming or saying or singing *argh* at a variety of pitches gets everything working. If you can, push your voice to the upper and lower extremities of its natural range, as this will help you use it more effectively, adding more color and variety, all things that will help engage the listeners.

For very significant presentations, perhaps an awards ceremony where there are a lot of tricky names to pronounce (see Chapter 12), you may want to include some of the articulation exercises in Chapter 6. This is especially important if you know certain combinations of syllables that feature in personal and company names cause you problems when you try to speak them out loud. Almost everyone has something they routinely stumble over in speech, so pick an exercise that helps you overcome your weaknesses and avoid those pronunciation tripwires.

Visualization

Visualizing your success with people applauding, laughing, or agreeing to a sale is another very successful technique that can be developed over time. This can start when you begin to prepare a presentation by creating mental snapshots to carry with you to recall just before you go on the stage. Imagine the audience applauding you loudly when you finish, laughing at your humor, their rapt attention during the presentation or them praising you afterward. This helps build confidence and self-belief.

This technique can be extended, especially if you have difficulty imagining yourself being successful on the stage. If you cannot visualize yourself, then pretending you are going to be an actor playing the part of a confident speaker may be a technique worth exploring. Many experienced actors can be strangely shy and diffident when not striding across the stage or in front of the cameras, and there are professional speakers who have built their success around almost creating another persona for when they are on the stage.

Others find recalling a good feeling associated with high self-esteem, such as when being praised by their boss, also works well. They say to themselves: "That is how I want to feel when I come off the stage" and work toward that objective.

Visualization should ideally start well before the big day. As you are creating a presentation, you should start to visualize what successful delivery of it will look and feel like. Capturing part of that feeling and recalling it before you go on stage will boost your performance.

One route not to take when seeking ways of relaxing before a presentation is the route to the bar. Alcohol may seem an obvious way to calm your nerves, and will often be suggested by colleagues who are trying to be helpful, but it rarely helps. For every little contribution you think it may make toward relaxing you, it is also threatening the quality and authority of your presentation. You need to be 100 percent in control on the stage, 100 percent on top of your game, and 100 percent focused on everything you have put into preparing your presentation. A quick drink beforehand will ensure you fall short of those ambitious targets.

Above all, do not be late. Nothing impairs your ability to be relaxed more than arriving late and flustered. Not only could you have missed your rehearsal slot, but all that preparation aimed at getting those butterflies flying in an effective formation will have been wasted: they will be flying off in all directions.

Relaxation Checklist

- Make time for yourself and use it well.
- Breathing deeply and filling your lungs with air.
- Reduce muscle tension by using simple exercises.
- Visualize your success and carry that mental image with you onto the stage.
- Never be late.

CHAPTER 4

Content Versus Style

I've learned that people will forget what you said, people will forget what you did, but people will never forget how you made them feel.
—Maya Angelou, American poet, singer, and civil rights activist

There is plenty of research that shows audiences respond much more to style than to content. Up to 90 percent of a presentation's impact can be attributed to the speaker's voice and body language, a frightening thought for the inexperienced speaker.[1] Put another way, content is not king when it comes to public speaking: you have to work on the style too (see Figure 4.1).

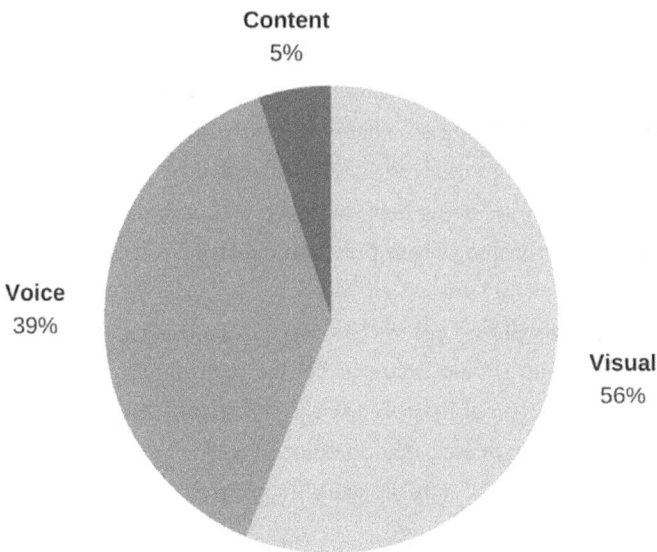

Content
5%

Voice
39%

Visual
56%

Figure 4.1 The speaker's impact

---

[1] Stuart, C. 1988. *Effective Speaking*, 137. London: Pan Books.

The visual element in the graph also includes slides, videos, and other external elements of a presentation, about which more later.

We all lose interest in a speech if the speaker talks so quietly we strain to hear, or if they stand perfectly still, clutching the sides of the lectern, or never look at us. Similarly, a monotone voice destroys an audience's interest in even the most fascinating of subject matter. So, style matters.

However, this is not necessarily the complete triumph of style over substance, although there have been many great speakers who can hold an audience enthralled, but leave them wondering afterward what they actually said. What it does say is that you might have the best content in the world, but if you put it across badly or inappropriately, it will be wasted.

Developing an engaging style that reflects your personality and builds on your own strengths has to be a key objective of anyone stepping out from behind their desk to take to the stage. The next three chapters break down some of the basic elements of style and stagecraft that people who want to be effective speakers, who are praised, and invited back should focus on: stance, eyes, gestures, and voice.

Once you have mastered those basics, you can develop a distinctive style of your own that you will be able to rely on in a variety of circumstances.

The key thing to keep in mind as you work through these basic elements is to keep building on what works for you.

Listen to other speakers, especially the good ones. Ask yourself if there is something they are doing that you could take and make work for yourself. If there is, put that in your presentational toolkit too, and try it when the right opportunity arises.

Often, you will find yourself reflecting on a really good presentation and thinking you should aspire to be like that one day. That is a great ambition, but be careful not to attempt to be something you are not by trying an approach or style that does not sit well with your own personality. Grab the bits you can make work for yourself, and just admire those you cannot see yourself using.

Never forget that presenting is an intensely practical art. Inexperienced speakers can read all the theory in the world, but unless they take it onto the stage and see whether it works for them, they will never know what they need to do to succeed. Take what you read here and elsewhere, and what you learn from watching others, and put it into practice. Do not try everything new all at once, but adopt a few new stylistic techniques at a time and work on making those work.

An ideal opportunity to do this comes when you have to make the same speech to different audiences, as you might have to on a road show tour or a sales presentation to a series of clients. You can polish up phrases, work on the pauses, gestures, voice, and so on. By concentrating on improving these things, you should also avoid the obvious pitfall of sounding stale by day five.

The key is to build up a reliable toolkit of presentational and rhetorical devices that work well for you and your audiences. Sometimes, this will mean being courageous enough to ask them or trusted colleagues what they thought, even down to asking them about specific elements of your presentation.

There are some decisions on style that must be made before you step out in front of your audience such as what should you wear.

This is often overlooked, but it is a key element of any speech, as the audience spends a long time looking at you. If there is a live video relay onto a big screen, it becomes even more important, as audiences are easily distracted by silly things.

The key to choosing what to wear is to pick something that will enhance your authority and not undermine it. Be cautious and do not be clever. Think very carefully before departing from conventional business (or evening) attire. If you opt to wear something distinctive, you will be setting yourself apart from your audience, almost certainly raising their expectations of how you will perform. They will judge you harshly if you fail to fulfill those expectations. Of course, the flipside of that particular coin is that, if you match or exceed what the audience expects, you will be hailed a great success. It is something to consider as you gain more experience (see Figure 4.2).

You may need to consider the color of the stage backdrops for some events if you are likely to wear a strong color yourself. You neither want to clash with the color of a stage backdrop of match it so closely that you seem to merge into it. Chequered, striped, and geometric patterned shirts and ties should be avoided if video relay or recording is being used, as those watching on screens or viewing it later will experience what is called strobing when patterns give the appearance of shimmering. It is unnecessarily distracting.

Figure 4.2 If you are going to wear something distinctive make sure you can live up to the expectation that creates

Source: Credit: Infopro Digital

For men, what to wear for a business presentation used to be easy. A business suit, plain shirt, and tie was all that was required. Nowadays, dress standards are more casual, and there is a greater range of choice. Think of how you want the audience to view you and how your natural style, the subject and content of your presentation can be most appropriately complimented by your choice of attire.

You may also need to consider how you might compare with other speakers at a conference. You might think that going without a tie might suggest you are forward-looking, modern, and trendy, but find yourself completely outshone in that regard by the guy wearing jeans, a t-shirt, and with a pony tail.

For women, many of the same considerations apply, but they are often judged—harshly and unfairly—even more on what they wear. Dress to reinforce your message, not distract from it. Women also need to be aware of other factors that will not present a problem for men. For instance, short skirts are not a good idea on an elevated stage with the audience close to the front. High heels if there are large steps to and from the stage or if it has a polished wood floor need to be managed carefully too.

Men might want to think twice about wearing white or brightly colored socks if they are on an elevated stage where feet are in the direct eye line of the front row. That is not to say never wear them, but just do not be surprised when someone comments afterward on your socks, rather than your speech.

These things may seem small, but they can distract from your presentation.

For many years, I introduced a major awards ceremony for the insurance industry at London's Royal Albert Hall, and when I did, I wore a white tuxedo rather than the traditional black dinner suit of the then overwhelmingly male audience. Over a decade later, people still remember the white jacket, but cannot recall a word I ever said. That is fine because it was an event that was about visual and musical spectacle, as well as the substance of the awards. It was a very conscious choice on my part, and that is what any distinctive attire must be.

Above all, be yourself, and make sure you feel comfortable.

Take all the advice in the next two chapters on board, but do not forget to be yourself. Too often, people who go on speaker training courses have the personality coached out of them with over-prescriptive advice on how to stand, speak, and incorporate gestures into their presentations. This should never be the aim of training or coaching.

Always try to project something of your own personality from the platform by using gestures and intonation that is as natural to you as possible and enables you to feel that bit more comfortable when in the spotlight.

This will help the audience warm toward you.

Style Checklist

- Create a style that works for you and is adaptable.
- Seize opportunities to practice and perfect your style.
- Think about what to wear. Is it enhancing your message or distracting from it?
- Be yourself.

CHAPTER 5

Components of Style

People travel to wonder at the height of mountains, at the huge waves of the sea, at the long courses of rivers, at the vast compass of the ocean, at the circular motion of the stars: and they pass by themselves without wondering.

—St Augustine of Hippo, 4th/5th century theologian

What all the research that highlights how much style matters really tells us is that you can have great content, beautifully structured, and well-argued, but if it is not delivered well, it will not be effective and the audience will not remember it. There are some caveats to the 90 percent style matters most rule, as it is only a crude average. More sophisticated audiences expecting a presentation containing technical, legal, or academic insights will not be so reliant on the style of a presentation to absorb the information. However, the growing number of complaints from university undergraduates in the United Kingdom about boring, uninspiring lectures shows that, even in a teaching environment, people expect a more engaging presentational style than might have previously been the norm.[1] This finding has been similar to the studies published elsewhere in the world.[2]

If we can make people remember us, they are much more likely to remember our message, and the best foundations for that are our own personalities and characteristics. This may sound off-putting for the

---

[1] Freeman, S., S.L. Eddy, M. McDonough, M.K. Smith, N. Okoroafor, H. Jordt, and M.P. Wenderoth. May 2014. "Active Learning Increases Student Performance in Science, Engineering and Mathematics." *Proceedings of the National Academy of Sciences* 111, no. 23, pp. 8410–15.

[2] Lectures Don't Work But We Keep Using Them. Times Higher Education Supplement, London. November 2013.

timid, novice speaker. One of the key elements of any presentation that helps an audience listen to it and remember it is sincerity. This is not just about telling the truth, it is about being true to yourself on the stage.

We can make this less intimidating by breaking style down into four separate elements that the inexperienced speaker can work on one at a time, slowly building an *act* that is engaging, and crucially, effective in putting across a variety of content in different situations. Those four key elements are:

- Stance
- Eyes
- Gestures
- Voice

Let us examine those in turn.

Stance

You set your style from the moment you step up to the rostrum. Eyes will be on you, and this is a key moment in any presentation. No one can hear your heart pounding, feel your sweaty palms, or know your mouth has dried up, so do not let your face give away your fear. Unless it is an especially solemn occasion, such as a eulogy at a funeral, try to smile when you get up, as this sends out a signal that you are looking forward to talking to the audience. They will subconsciously reciprocate by feeling they are looking forward to hearing from you.

As you go up to the rostrum look confident, regardless of how you actually feel. Walk with purpose. If you have practiced your *walk to the rostrum*, this should come naturally and convey a sense that you are comfortable on the stage. It is the first, tentative step in building what people often refer to as *stage presence*, which is about you dominating the stage and not the stage overwhelming you.

Have your papers ready, so you do not have to shuffle them when you get to the rostrum. These first few seconds of the audience's attention are so important you do not want to waste them by shuffling through your script or cards. If you have to use a remote control to change slides, make sure this is immediately to hand if it is not fixed to the lectern. Anything, such as looking around for such a basic piece of equipment, that detracts from creating the impression that you know what you are doing and know why you are on the stage erodes the audiences' belief and confidence in a speaker. These small things matter.

Stand up straight and look out into the hall first before looking at your notes or the screen. You want to reinforce the belief you have started to build with the audience that you want to be there and that you want to engage with them. If for some reason the audience is still noisy or restless, hold this look for a few seconds. People are much more likely to settle down if they feel you are looking at them.

Do not apologize. If you mention your nervousness or apologize for any problem you think you might have with your presentation, you will probably be calling the audience's attention to something most of them have not noticed. These first few seconds are about building a confident image that says: "I want to be here and am going to do the best job I possibly can for you." Do not throw it away unnecessarily.

Standing up straight is another important element in building that vital stage presence. It is all about making the audience think that you really want to be there and have not been pushed reluctantly into making a presentation you would rather someone else was doing, whatever the truth of the situation might be.

It helps some people to think of themselves as an old-fashioned puppet with a string attached to the top of their head, which is pulled taut to help them stand straight and tall.

Once you get into your presentation, do not rock from side-to-side or cross your legs as you speak. Even slightly bending one leg at the knee creates a poor impression. It twists your body slightly to one side, which you will then compensate for by leaning slightly the other way at the waist. To an audience, this just looks causal and certainly not business-like.

The ideal position—at least to start with—is to have your feet slightly apart with knees, hips and shoulders all neatly aligned as you stand up straight. Obviously, if you are going to move around as you speak, you will move from this position, but even then, you should remind yourself of the need to periodically return to this effective basic stance.

If you are particularly tall or particularly short, check the lectern height and the position of the microphones carefully beforehand as adjusting them when you are at the rostrum looks unprofessional. If some adjustments need to be made between speakers, ideally these should be done by a member of the production team and not left to the speaker. This definitely applies to anyone with a disability who cannot speak from a conventional standing position. All of the adjustments should be made by the production staff before you come on stage, and if appropriate, easy wheelchair access should be available and have formed part of your pre-event test of the *route to the rostrum*.

Most of this advice is about what to do when you are standing. That is because it is almost always the best option, even with relatively small groups. Sitting at a table gives you more excuse to fiddle with pens and papers and look down at your notes. It is sometimes appropriate for sales presentations or when you are opening a roundtable discussion or debate, so think about how you are going to create that moment of maximum opportunity just before you start your presentation: sit up straight, look around the table, and pause before speaking.

Eyes

Not looking at an audience is one of the most obvious signs of nerves and fear in a speaker, so we all need to work on eye contact. This can sound quite intimidating, so it is best to think of it as holding a conversation. It seems very strange if someone is talking to us face-to-face and does not look at us. Eye contact signals engagement and interest. It is exactly the same with larger groups of people, except that, with large groups, we have to create an illusion of engagement and meaningful eye contact.

A basic, simple approach is to identify no more than three points in the auditorium that you can use as reference points to *work* the room: one near the front, one in the middle, and one at the back. If it is a wide auditorium, the front and middle points could be slightly to either side. One point must always be at the back, as focusing on the people furthest away from you will help you with voice projection. Microphones only amplify your voice; they do relatively little to project it, so this is something you have to work on. The people at the back must feel you are speaking to them, not merely listening to your voice.

As your speech progresses, you can turn to these points, thus guaranteeing that more or less everyone in the room feels you have spoken to them. Do not do this mechanically, but in a relaxed and natural manner, and try to find a few people you have sufficient confidence to look in the eye: they will remember more of what you are saying.

Different-shaped rooms and stages present a mixture of challenges when it comes to building meaningful eye contact.

A common problem is a raised stage with the first few rows of the audience close to the front of the stage. If people have filled up the front rows, it is easy to forget that they are there and almost spend the whole of a presentation talking over their heads. Remember to look (down) at them occasionally, so they feel engaged in the presentation too.

Wide rooms with the speaker positioned well to one side of a stage also create the potential for a section of the audience to be overlooked. If you find yourself on a stage in a room laid out in this way, again you have to make a special effort to engage the members of the audience sitting furthest away from you.

Think of your eyes as delivering the message. It is not going to reach the recipients safely unless you look them in the eye. This is most effective if you deliver complete sentences to the same person or group of people. People can be left feeling subconsciously short-changed if you look at them when you start a sentence, but look away to deliver the end of it to someone else. Think of it as throwing a ball to someone. You look up and engage them, so they know the ball is coming, and you watch its flight until it lands safely in the hands of the recipient.

It is so important that you look at the audience from time-to-time. This means you need to feel comfortable and confident with your presentation. If you are using a full script, you will have to make a conscious effort to do this. And, you should have certain passages almost committed to memory so that you can look up for long enough to ensure a few sentences at a time are delivered with meaningful eye contact.

If the script is on an autocue, then you will be helped enormously in overcoming the challenge of sticking to a carefully crafted script while trying to maintaining the illusion of eye contact with an audience. However, this can create its own problems, depending on how the autocues are positioned in relation to the rostrum and the shape of the room. If the autocues are fairly far apart, there is a danger that, in turning from one to the other, the speaker effectively ignores the audience sitting down at the center of the room. Engaging them will require turning away from the autocue for time-to-time. There is more advice on using autocues in Chapter 9.

If you are speaking with slides, then be especially careful not to fall into the all too common trap of talking to the screen and not to the audience. This quickly disengages an audience from what the speaker is saying, as it appears to the audience that the speaker is more interested in their own slides than in them. You should ensure that you can see the slides on a small screen in front of you so that you do not feel compelled to turn to a screen behind you to check that each transition has completed satisfactorily.

Gestures

Gestures are one of the hardest elements to get right. The key is to look natural even though you may have carefully rehearsed what gestures you are going to use and where in your presentation you are going to use them.

There is a balance to be struck between looking too wooden, missing the opportunity to engage the audience with carefully chosen gestures, and being so hyperactive that the audience becomes distracted by flaying arms and constant movement. It is often said that some people talk with their hands, and learning how to do this effectively on the stage is a crucial element in the armory of every top-class presenter.

There are several things you can think about when you are preparing a presentation or speech, which will help you get the balance between being static and visually uninteresting while not being hyperactive or feeling uncomfortable.

Start by learning how to use your arms and hands to emphasize points. This is not just about pointing, but about creating small visual signals that help reinforce your spoken words. For instance:

- Making a fist if you are talking about confronting someone, taking up the fight on an issue.
- Holding out a hand if you are making a point about partnership or reaching out to a group or a firm.

- Using both hands to create a circle when you are talking about the entirety of a project or issue.
- Holding the palm of one (or both) hands up to signify that something should stop.

There are plenty more, some of which will come naturally to you; others that will seem more contrived.

Plan where you can use these appropriate gestures, even drawing little pictures in your script to remind you if that helps. No one else can see your script, so they will not know they have been planned and rehearsed.

As a good general rule, gestures using the arms should be used between the waist (or top of the rostrum) and chin. Be especially careful not to raise your hands in front of your mouth as this is an obvious inhibition to getting your message across to an audience.

Focus on creating slow, measured arms movements, holding the position so that the audience understands the visual signal. This also conveys a calm confidence and authority to the audience. Jerky, fast arm movements should be used sparingly for when you want to convey aggression and anger or excessive excitement.

If you are using slides, occasionally point toward something on one of them without turning completely away from the audience. Occasionally, half-turning toward the screen is fine, but turning your back on the audience must be avoided. If the stage layout and demands of the presentation—picking out some specific detail on a graph for instance—require you to turn away to point at a screen, make sure the microphone(s) can still pick up your voice or stop talking as you turn to look at the screen.

Facial gestures are also effective, especially if there is a video relay either to a big screen behind you or to smaller screens dotted around the hall if it is a large room or has problems with sightlines, such as pillars. Even without a video relay, it is surprising how aware people are of facial gestures even if they are a long way from the stage. Obviously, these cannot be overdone, as they could easily seem too contrived but quizzical, stern, welcoming, or other appropriate looks from time-to-time help keep an audience engaged with a speaker.

Resist the temptation to fiddle with your hands and keep them away from your face or your hair. Nervous gestures that have become deeply embedded in your personality, such as running a hand through your hair, are fine on the stage very occasionally, but should not be repeated frequently. If you feel this could be a problem, then you must focus on eliminating them when you are making a presentation.

Remember not to grip the lectern as if your life depends on making sure it does not run away. You will quickly become very static in addition to generating unwanted tension up your arms.

If you are unsure about how your natural stance and gestures appear to others, then there is no substitute for asking for input from people who have seen and heard you speak. Looking for feedback is essential for any presenter who wants to improve, but is often hard to take on board. We are asking people to comment on aspects of our appearance that are quite personal to us: how we stand, how we move, and how we speak. It is something that you will have to learn to be brave about if you want to master the art of public speaking.

Often, the best place to start is to ask relatives, partners, and trusted colleagues for constructive feedback—and the emphasis must be on *constructive*. Feedback expressed in excessively negative terms is no good to anyone. It will undermine fragile confidence and push those nerves up to performance-crippling levels. It is important to pick the right people to give you feedback and advice.

Conversely, do not ask people who are just going to flatter you: constructive honesty is what you need.

Videoing yourself rehearsing or, when it is available, watching a recording of yourself speaking can be extremely helpful, especially once you have a clear idea of what it is you want to improve. Often, we are our own harshest critics, and watching ourselves can be very painful, which is why having a clear idea of what it is you want to work on and improve is helpful when using a video.

You may want to review how particular gestures work. Do they seem appropriate? Do they look natural and authoritative? Do they help put your message across?

You may want to check your posture. Am I standing up straight? Am I rocking from side-to-side? Do I move too much or too little? Am I looking out at the audience enough?

By focusing on just a few key points at a time, you are much more likely to find reviewing a video of yourself a beneficial exercise. The next time you speak, you should then focus on just those aspects of your style. Trying to do too much at the same time rarely ends in success, as you will find you have given yourself too much to think about in what we know is a supremely stressful environment.

Voice

It goes without saying that your voice is the key element in creating your style, and so we devote the whole of the next chapter to how to make the most of your voice.

Style: The Basics

- Remember all eyes are on you from the moment you stand up, so make the most of that moment.
- Stand tall, look out at the audience.
- Use your eyes to engage the audience and work the room.
- Incorporate appropriate gestures to add visual interest.
- Ask for honest, but constructive feedback.

CHAPTER 6

Making the Most of Your Voice

The Human voice is the most perfect instrument of all.
—Arvo Pärt, Estonian composer

Always remember that, in oral presentations, voice is the most important factor. No amount of gestures, slides, or even brilliant content can compensate for a poor voice. This is what the inexperienced speaker should concentrate on most of all. If your voice is interesting, varied, and appropriately animated, people will stay engaged. If it is dull, monotone, and flat, their attention will quickly wander.

The starting point has to be listening to yourself. Most people find this an excruciating experience, but it is one that no one who wants to be a public speaker should run away from. Hardly anyone's voice sounds to others as they hear it themselves, so it is essential that you hear yourself as your audience does.

Record yourself speaking normally, as well as reading some poetry, prose, or drama, and maybe, as you think, you might speak when giving a speech if you feel you already have a distinct public speaking style. This will give you some basic benchmarks for improving and identifying specific aspects of your voice that you need to work on. If you can do this with the help of a partner, friend, or colleague, then, once the initial embarrassment has passed, it will be easier to critically assess your voice and identify the key elements to develop.

All of our voices sound different. They are part of our personality and the starting point for any speaker who has to be to build on their personality. For this reason, different accents in themselves are not a bad thing. They only become a problem if they inhibit the ability of a listener to absorb the message the speaker is delivering. Some regional accents in the

British Isles, United States, and other English-speaking countries are very distinctive, often incorporating features from local dialects (which are not the same as accents). Intelligibility is the key, and accents only become a problem when an audience cannot understand the speaker. If you have a strong regional accent, identify those aspects of it that others from outside your region might have problems understanding and focus, on making those clearer for mixed audiences.

Similar considerations apply to people for whom English is a second language. Working with other people, identify those aspects of your accent and pronunciation that a significant proportion of an average audience might struggle to understand. This is where you need to start improving the clarity. Using the articulation exercises later in this chapter will be a great help in achieving this.

Above all, you need to focus on how much you vary the pitch and pace. Variation of these two key factors is what makes a voice more interesting to the listener. Usually, for the novice speaker, this means stepping out of comfort zones.

Listen to how you speak, especially when reading some text, and challenge yourself by asking whether you really brought it alive, whether the key words with the most important meanings really stood out for the listener, and whether, if asked to speak like that for 30 minutes, it would be sufficiently varied in pitch and pace to keep someone listening.

That should give you your starting point for improvement. So, precisely where do we start?

The human voice is a remarkable and complex instrument. It is not just about vocal chords, but about the whole upper part of your body. Learning to fill your lungs with air and expand your chest is important because the chest is a sound box and is where you need to work on getting as much of the sound as possible to come from. Your throat and the vocal chords it contains needs to be looked after by exercising them properly and learning to relax them. Your mouth and tongue play a crucial part in forming words and sounds, essential if what you say it to be truly intelligible. Even the rest of your head is important because it has several resonators (spaces) that help change the tone of your voice. If you put your fingers on your temples lightly and hum loudly, you should feel small vibrations: that is your voice resonating in your skull.

What we have to do is take all of those fantastic tools and use them to maximum effect.

This is not just a question of focusing on physical exercises. They can do a lot, but the real benefits and your transformation from an adequate public speaker to an outstanding one can only be achieved if you have the right mindset. You should be challenging yourself to take your voice further than it has ever been before: higher, lower, faster, slower, louder, and softer. Keep this in mind as you review the physical exercises that will help you.

Filling your lungs, breathing deeply, and expanding your chest are vital and should be the starting point. By focusing on lifting your voice from the diaphragm, you will develop a richer, deeper sound that will project more effectively. You will also take some of the strain off your vocal chords, essential if you expect to speak for a long time or several times over the space of a few days, as a politician touring the country during an election campaign might.

Some people are blessed with naturally loud voices and seem to master the techniques of breathing deeply and using their diaphragm to help project their voice with ease. The rest of us have to work on it. Projecting your voice is not about shouting. That would quickly get very wearing for the listener and hard on your vocal chords. It is about combining those techniques of speaking to the back of the room and to all of the people in it with sourcing the voice from within your diaphragm, rather than your throat.

Singers are trained to breathe, filling their lungs before opening their mouths. When they do open their mouths, they are usually projecting the sound from deep within their body, not from their throat. If they want to reach very high notes, then they will use the natural resonators in their head to similarly project the sound to the audience. In essence, these are the techniques you must master. In particular, you should avoid tensing your throat muscles, not easy when you are nervous.

There are whole books written on breathing, speaking, and singing exercises, but a simple mix will help most people improve quite quickly and enable them to sustain that improvement. There are many simple voice exercises that can help with different problems or just help you get ready to make the perfect speech.

Work on breathing in deeply and letting the air out slowly, first through your nose and then with a hiss or a hum. Get into the habit of doing this regularly before you speak, repeating the exercise several times extending the exhalation period each time.

Now, think about how you might work on the pitch.

When you are practicing a speech, try focusing on lifting your voice from within your diaphragm, rather than speaking from your throat. It will probably feel strange at first, but after a while, it will become more natural and is the first, crucial ingredient to stretching the pitch of your voice.

Stepping outside of your comfort zone is difficult, but stretching your voice requires you to be brave and bold in the way you approach this challenge. You can start to do this quite simply by speaking out loud, preferably to another human being, first in as low a pitch as you can and then in as high a pitch as you can. This is not about looking down to the ground or up to the sky. Indeed, you should try to keep your head still while you do this, as you will not be looking up and down like that when you are on the stage.

When taking it lower than you ever imagined, you might concentrate on lifting the sound from deep within your body. At the other extreme, when taking your voice very high, think of it coming out of the top of your head.

Mix up the pitches: start high and finish low, start low and finish high. The aim is to take your voice to places it has probably never been before—or at least only in extreme situations. Of course, you will not be using the very extremes when you are on the stage, but by demonstrating to yourself that your voice has more natural variety than you may have imagined, you will find yourself naturally varying the pitch more.

Once you have explored where you can go with the pitch, you should turn to the pace.

Pace is, in theory at least, easier to practice varying. You can take a passage and read it slower and then faster and then mix up changes of pace. Again, it is important that you take yourself outside your comfort zones by reading it ridiculously slowly and then absurdly fast.

When you read it slowly, try to concentrate on joining the words up so it is not just a succession of words that have no connection. What you speak should still have a sense of direction to the listener.

When you go fast, focus on diction and clarity. A lot of this will be about quickly changing the shape of your mouth and the position of your tongue and is really good practice for speaking with greater clarity and focusing on words and syllables that you might have difficulty in pronouncing.

Using these exercises will also help you develop greater control over your voice when stress levels are high.

When you are nervous, your voice normally rises in pitch and quickens in pace, but not always in the right way and not because you are in control of the changes. Pitch often rises because the neck becomes tense, and this constricts the voice in the vocal chords. Not only does this make the voice sound thinner, it also puts greater strain on the vocal chords. The nervous acceleration of pace makes a presentation sound hurried, even garbled. You must try to guard against these obvious pitfalls, but you need to be aware of how prone you are to them first. Doing these exercises will gradually give you a greater sense of control over your voice and should make you realize just how much more you can do with it.

It is an unfortunate scientific fact that a high-pitched woman's voice is harder to listen to for long periods than a man's voice or a woman with a naturally lower voice, so women have to be particularly careful on this count.[1] The best women newsreaders have lower than average voices, and the former British Prime Minister Margaret Thatcher had intense voice coaching to help her lower the pitch of her voice quite dramatically when she became the leader of the Conservative Party in 1975, something that actually featured in the 2011 film of her life, Iron Lady.

The simple relaxation exercises discussed earlier (in Chapter 3) can help control both pitch and pace, so think of these as helping your voice too. Eliminating tension is very important, never more so than when you have to speak for a long time—by which we mean anything over 20 minutes—as a tense neck and throat quickly dries up, making your voice hoarse and uncomfortable.

Having tried these exercises, now it is important to apply their beneficial effects in more realistic situations than the absurd extremes you

---

[1] Tickle, L. July 9, 2018. "Terrified of Public Speaking? Start with What You Really Want to Say?" *The Guardian*. https://theguardian.com/lifeandstyle/2018/apr/09/terrified-of-public-speaking-start-with-what-you-really-want-to-say

should have been taking them to by following the advice above. At the same time, you need to start paying attention to color and tone.

Try reading some poetry or dramatic prose out loud and recording it. Play it back and ask yourself whether you could do more to vary the pitch, pace, and tone of your voice to make it sound more interesting.

Try to imagine that you are reading to a child or a room full of children. There are two ways you might approach this, one is to keep it calm in order to them send them to sleep, while the other is to excite and engage them. Try both, as this will help you to vary the pitch and tone much more. When it comes to the more animated version, think hard about which words need to be brought alive and stress them with those variations of pitch. Look for the colorful words, strong adjectives, active verbs, expressions of emotion, and so on.

Poetry, prose, and speeches from plays are also very useful tools for learning to build meaningful pauses and using variations in the pitch and pace to good effect.

Look for passages that need greater excitement and inject more pace into them, but remember to seek out those passages where the reading needs to be calmer and slow the pace down. Work out where you can carefully insert pauses to help achieve this.

If you struggle with where to pause, do it in a very structured way to start with: insert a short pause where there is a comma, a slightly longer one where there is a full stop, and an even longer one for a paragraph. It sounds a little formulaic, and you would never apply it that rigidly in a real-life situation, but it will help you understand how to use pauses. In particular, they are a great way of slowing down and lowering the pitch after a spell of excitement, or, having set out the background to an argument or a particular point, a pause can be a way of then coming in with greater energy and excitement—simply conveyed by a faster pace and higher pitch.

You need to think about how you carry this variation through an entire speech. It is no good having the most brilliant, energetic, animated start if this leaves you nowhere to go at the end.

One of the most challenging speeches in this regard in all drama is Henry V's speech before Harfleur from William Shakespeare's play Henry V (Act 3, scene 1).

It begins:

"Once more unto the breach, dear friends, once more;
Or close the wall up with our English dead."

But, then continues for another 30 lines before finishing with:

"Follow your spirit, and upon this charge
Cry 'God for Harry, England, and Saint George!'"

Clearly, the rousing conclusion has to have at least as much impact as the dramatic and arresting beginning. The world's greatest actors take a variety of approaches to achieving this, and it is worth reviewing some of them on YouTube (see Figure 6.1).

Pauses are also important in verbal communication because they aid intelligibility, giving audiences a chance to absorb a point before you move on to the next one.

It is worth spending time mastering the art of the pause. A useful technique to help develop the use of pauses effectively is to stand behind a chair (with or without somebody in it) and read the passage out loud,

Figure 6.1 Laurence Olivier as Henry V delivering the famous speech before Harfleur

Source: Credit: You Tube https://youtube.com/watch?v=q6pWPiNUiyg

tapping the back of the chair or the shoulder of the person at the end of each sentence or passage while you pause. Vary the length of the pauses so that the paragraphs have longer pauses and so on. It is always best to involve another person because it stops you skipping parts of the exercise or being too perfunctory in how you approach it.

Listen for obvious bad habits such as letting your voice trail away at the end of a sentence. This is a common and serious failing. Ask yourself: does every sentence sound the same? If it does, the monotony will quickly send your listeners to sleep. Work on variation by starting some sentences (artificially) high and taking them down in pitch, while with other sentences start them low, making a point of lifting the very end of the sentence up a notch or two. It will sound strange, but it will help you get used to injecting greater variety into your presentations.

You must also work out whether you are putting genuine emphasis on the right words and phrases. Take the passage(s) you have been practicing and underline the key words and phrases, then re-read them aloud several times trying different techniques to bring them alive. Think of this as coloring in the obviously colorful words—the key adjectives and active verbs in particular. Make them stand out orally as you would visually if you were highlighting them on the page.

When you listen to yourself, check that you are not going *um* and *ah* when you should be pausing quietly. This quickly becomes very distracting for the listener, and if you are doing it, you need to work hard—through practice—to eliminate it. Speakers, either consciously or subconsciously, often feel they have to fill every second and fraction of a second with a sound. You do not. Silence can be very effective too.

Listen carefully for any problems with articulation. Passages that you try speaking artificially fast often reveal words and syllables that you have a tendency to stumble over. Are there certain syllables that get lost or which you tend to swallow? This is not unusual, as almost everyone has certain words, sounds, or letters they find hard to pronounce. There is almost certainly an exercise that can help you overcome the problem.

Mastering the different sounds letters make is also important for conveying the meaning of words and passages. Think about how different vowel sounds can help communicate different emotions. If too many of your vowels sound the same or indistinct, then finding exercises that work on these is essential. Often, this is about thinking about the shape your mouth makes to create different vowel sounds. The first exercise below—"Unique New York, New York Unique"—illustrates this point well.

Clear articulation of consonants is something that is also important. They provide the structure of words. If they are not clear, people will find it hard to understand key words and phrases. In most English-speaking countries, dropping certain consonants is taken as an indication of poor education, and like it or not, leads audiences to make instant judgments about the speaker—probably not ideal for business speakers wanting to be taken seriously.

Top-class presenters, actors, newsreaders, and speakers use articulation exercises all the time. They help get the jaw and tongue moving and ensure that their words are clear and convey the right meaning and emotions.

There are a whole series of *pitter, patter, tittle, tattle, cupid keeper* exercises that help. Just say the pairs of words as fast as you can, repeating many times. You can work out pairs of words that challenge you for yourself. Having found some that work, you can go on to create a short warm-up routine incorporating the syllables you want to focus on with other articulation exercises.

You should also work on the tone by thinking of the different inflexions you can use with the same word to convey different emotions.

Hello: pleasantly surprised to see someone.
Hello: pleased to see someone, but not surprised.
Hello: cautious about seeing someone.
Hello: annoyed at seeing someone.
Hello: irritated by seeing someone you did not expect to be there.
Hello: pleased to see a dear friend.

The variation in emotion will be embodied in the sound of your vowels, which is why it is so important to make sure that you have a good range of vowel sounds.

When it comes to improving the clarity of your diction, there is a mixture of tongue-twisters and structured exercises available. Pick and choose which articulation exercises work best for you and especially help address any weaknesses you might have. It is good to have a few tongue-twisters and also a few warm-up exercises under your belt.

The following are a few of the best articulation exercises. As an actor, singer, presenter, or speaker, it is important to develop your articulation. If you are ever performing a classical text such as Shakespeare, you really need to have clear diction. The same applies to any script—such as for an awards ceremony—that contains a lot of names. The less familiar the audience is likely to be with the words you are using, the more important crystal-clear articulation becomes.

It is important to loosen up your jaw and tongue first as it is in your mouth that most of the different sounds that create words are made.

Draw circles in each cheek with the tip of the tongue. Aim to make the circles as perfect as possible. Once you have completed 10 in one direction, draw 10 more circles in the opposite direction. Do the same for the other cheek.

Rotate your chin five times in each direction, so you really stretch the big muscles either side of your jawbone.

Stretch your neck muscles by gently and slowly leaning your head as far toward each shoulder and holding it there for three seconds, alternating each side three or four times. Then, do the same by pressing your chin toward your chest and then leaning your head back as far as it will comfortably go.

Do these simple exercises first before trying some of the more popular articulation exercises. Here is a selection that addresses different sounds.

Unique New York
New York Unique

To sit in solemn silence in a dull dark dock
In a pestilential prison with a life-long lock
Awaiting the sensation of a short sharp shock
From a cheap and chippy chopper on a big black block.

Red leather, yellow leather.

She says she shall sew a sheet.
He sawed six sleek, slim, slender saplings in twain.

What a to do to die today,
at a minute or two to two,
a thing distinctly hard to say,
but a harder thing to do.
For they'll beat a tattoo at two today
a rat a tat at two,
and the dragon will come when he hears the drum
at a minute or two to two today
at a minute or two today.

She stood on the balcony,
inexplicably mimicking him hiccupping,
and amicably welcoming him home.

A big black bug bit a big black bear and the big black bear bleed blue
black blood.

Peter Piper picked a peck of pickled peppers; a peck of pickled peppers Peter Piper picked.

In Tooting two tutors astute
Tried to tute a Duke on a flute
But duets so gruelling
End only in duelling
When tutors astute toot the flute.

Lesser leather never weathered lesser wetter weather.

Whenever the weather is cold, whenever the weather is hot. We'll
weather the weather whatever the weather whether we like it or not.

I scream, you scream, we all scream for ice-cream.

Once you feel you have mastered the tongue-twisting elements of these exercises, you should work on saying the phrases with meaning so that the sense (such as it is) of them is also clearly conveyed.

Key Tips for Using Your Voice Well

- Vary the pace. Do not rush, except when you mean to. Stay in control.
- Speak to the back of the hall.
- Learn to use pauses. Not every second has to be filled with a sound.
- Watch your pitch and introduce controlled variation.
- Take care with articulation.
- Do not let the ends of sentences trail away.
- Work on the color and tone to convey your meaning.

CHAPTER 7

Amplification and Microphones

But as I glared up at Hawkins, I realized he was only looking down at me. "You got my attention. Now what are you going to do with it?" He said into the microphone.

—Leah Spiegal, American singer/songwriter in Foolish Games

Amplification should be an obvious aid to help you use your voice more effectively. Most of the time, this is the case; occasionally, the opposite is true. It does not let you off the need to speak with clarity, interest, and good articulation, but does, of course, help with audibility, and up to a point, projection in a larger venue.

It is important that regular presenters are familiar with the range of microphones they will encounter. A presenter who walks onto a stage unsure of whether microphones are working, how to operate them, or whether the audience can hear them when they speak into the mic just makes themselves look amateurish and ill-prepared. In doing so, they instantly throw away that great opportunity to engage and build the audience belief that they are just the right person to listen to that only comes in those first few moments standing on the stage or behind the lectern.

Making sure you have the opportunity to do a proper sound check before you speak is an ideal way of building your confidence in a sound system. It will also help the sound engineers for the event to ensure that the microphone levels are adjusted for your voice.

Understanding how the different amplification options work and how they impact you as a speaker is as essential as all the other elements of preparation and practice so far discussed.

Microphones come in all shapes and sizes. They can be small, pencil-thin devices that are mounted on a rostrum; they can sit atop of a traditional stand; they can be large and put into your hand or small and pinned to your lapel. Some may have cables and wires; others may have none. Whatever type of microphone you find yourself working with, knowing its advantages, disadvantages, and limitations is important.

In the early days of your public speaking career, you really want as little to do with them as possible. Ideally, they should be mounted in front of you—and work. Remember to test them and get the sound engineers to test your volume levels. This should almost be automatic with any professionally run event. When you do a sound check, stand up straight—you should not be leaning into the microphone as the sound engineer should adjust the level to suit the speaker. If you have any doubts about how they work, whether you will be heard at the back of the hall, this is the time to ask. Do not wait until you are on the stage with the audience in front of you.

Of course, microphones mounted on a rostrum do restrict you to speaking from the rostrum. In most cases, this is likely to be absolutely fine and an option that works perfectly well for most speakers, especially those who are less experienced or who want to create an impression of authority. The formality of speaking from a rostrum lends a natural seriousness to a presentation.

It is now quite often the case even at an event where most of the speakers are static and speaking from a rostrum that the organizers opt to use small lapel, lavalier, or radio microphones (they go under various names). Usually, these are clipped to a lapel, shirt front, or tie and the wire between the microphone and the battery pack tucked away out of sight. If this is the option you are presented with, you need to think about where the wires will go so that they cannot be seen and are not hanging out, potentially distracting the audience, and where the battery pack goes.

Remember that you want to appear professional on the stage, looking and feeling comfortable. If you are uncertain about where to put a battery pack or end up with it making you feel uncomfortable, undecided about how best to hide the wires or constantly worrying about whether the microphone is picking up your voice your performance on the stage will be undermined.

Part of proper, thorough preparation should include asking about how you will be amplified and whether lapel mics will be used. If they are, you need to think about what you are going to wear.

Jackets are ideal for solving both problems. The internal pockets are ideal for putting the battery pack so that it will be secure and hide the wires. The mic can be clipped to a tie or lapel and the wires tucked inside the pocket with the battery pack. Always remember to remove or turn off any mobile phones as any signals it receives will interfere with the microphone, especially if it is close to it—and they can make an horrendous noise. Putting it on silent does not stop it receiving signals that interfere with the microphones (see Figures 7.1 and 7.2).

If you do not choose to wear a jacket, then the battery pack may be able to clip to the back of a trouser or skirt belt or go in a back pocket. The mic will be clipped to your shirt or blouse and the wire threaded through inside. If you choose to make a presentation without a jacket, you need to be comfortable with this.

More challenging is where to put and hide everything if you opt to wear a dress, especially if it does not have a belt. Many female television presenters solve this problem by clipping the battery pack onto their bra strap and threading the wire inside their dress up and over their shoulder to a mic clipped to the collar or neck of the dress. There is nothing wrong with this except that it does require somewhere discreet to make the necessary adjustments, and initially, you might feel slightly self-conscious.

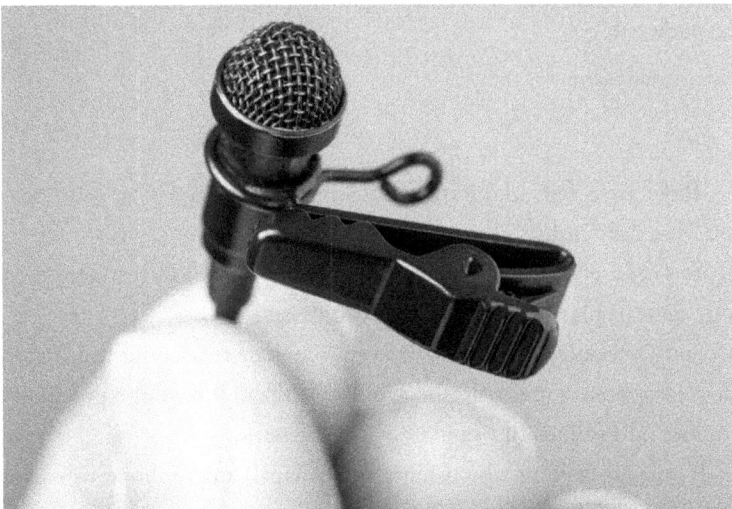

Figure 7.1 Lavalier (lapel) mic

Source: Credit: David Worsfold

**Figure 7.2 *Lapel mic and battery pack: make sure you know where
the pack will go***

Source: Credit: Samson

There are a few additional considerations that must be addressed if
you use a radio mic.

You must ensure that you do not strike it, perhaps in gestures beating
your chest or placing your hand on your heart.

Long necklaces, pendants, or even long hair that could brush across
the microphone should also be avoided as they all have the potential to
produce odd sounds that could distract listeners.

If you are going to be using a radio (lapel) microphone to create a
less formal physical context for your presentation by stepping out from
behind the rostrum, check how far you can wander across the stage with

it before causing problems with feedback. This could happen if you walk in front of the speakers or across the signal of another microphone that is turned on.

Also, check who is responsible for turning it on and off and who can hear what at what stage! Unless you are familiar with the equipment you are using, you should let the sound technicians turn on the microphone battery and leave yourself in their hands. You do not want to find yourself fiddling to find the on button moments before you step on the stage. However, this does mean that decisions about when to turn the microphone on and off are out of your hands. You have to trust the sound technicians, so be nice to them!

Radio mics can be helpful for experienced speakers wanting to create a more informal and accessible feel to a presentation. You cannot assume that these will be the default option for all events. If you know you want to use one, make sure you notify the organizers in advance as not all

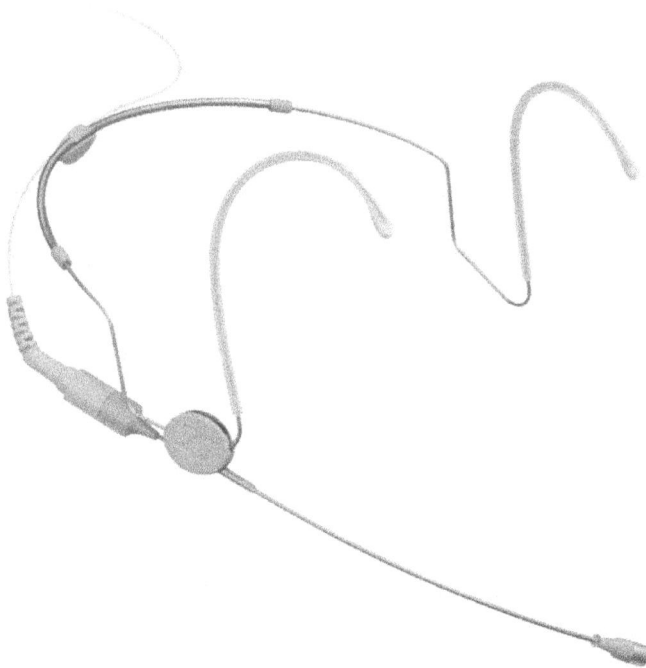

Figure 7.3 Typical headset mic

Source: Credit: Music Store Professional UK

sound engineers routinely carry them and the frequencies that can be used in the venue need to be checked.

Headsets are a variation on the radio mic theme, which have been used in entertainment and broadcasting for several years and are now creeping into the world of business presentations. They are slightly pretentious on a business conference platform and often make presenters who are not used to them feel very self-conscious.

If you are presented with one, you need to work with the sound engineer to ensure that it is fitted properly, sits well on your head without feeling uncomfortable, and that the wires to the battery pack are sensibly hidden. If you have not used one before, it is a good idea to walk around the stage with it on for a while, practice opening and closing your mouth, and turning your head so that you are 100 percent confident that it is in place and is not going to awkwardly poke you in the cheek or shake loose during your presentation.

Headset microphones also have battery packs and wires that need to be hidden (see Figure 7.3).

Finally, if you are using any style of radio mic, when you are doing your sound check, think about sightlines. If you are going to be walking around, you need to make sure you avoid walking in front of any projectors.

Most conference stages nowadays use back projection, so this will not be an issue, but sometimes, front projection is used, perhaps where there is not sufficient depth behind a stage set. The audience does not want to see a large black shadow of you strutting across the middle of a slide, so you will have to stay on one side of the stage.

You should also make sure you stay in the light (see Chapter 2). Often, conference sets have only limited stage lighting available, so the lighting technician will have carefully positioned it to get the best out of a modest rig. You need to ensure you know where the best light falls on your face. Walk around the stage, and if necessary, ask the technical crew where they think you can walk before your face disappears into a shadow.

If you have to hold a microphone, think hard about where your notes or cards are going to go and how you will manage them. Hand-held microphones are fine and are well-suited for some events. They are often the right choice when a sound engineer feels they need better directional control, perhaps because there is background noise. This is why you see them used for a lot of outside television broadcasts, especially at sporting events where crowd noise, stadium announcements, and music would all be picked up by a lapel mic.

Some hand-held microphones have leads; others are cordless. If you have a hand-held with a lead and want to walk around with it, make sure that you keep control of the lead as they have an awful tendency to wrap themselves around your ankles if left to their own devices.

Generally, a hand-held microphone should be held just in front of your chest and below your chin. You should speak across the top of it and be careful not to bring it too close to your mouth unless it has a decent foam or fur cover. If there is any background noise that you need to overcome, you will need to work with the sound engineer to judge how best to position the mic in order to ensure your voice comes through it. Normally, you do not need to hold it right in front of your mouth as some singers do. They are often using large microphones to mask lip-synching where they are miming to a pre-recorded sound track.

A hand-held microphone might be mounted on a simple stand. You need to make sure this is properly adjusted for your height before you go up to speak from it. Again, you should position it so that you can stand up straight and talk across the top of it. You should not have to lean into it. Occasionally, you might have to adjust the height if someone else has been using it before you. This is not ideal, but if you find yourself in that situation, make sure you know exactly how to adjust it—how to loosen it, move it up or down, and tighten it again.

Microphones do not let you off the need to project your voice, although they do ensure that you do not have to work too hard on the volume. Projection and volume are not the same thing, and even with good microphones, you must make sure you still work the room and talk to the people at the back and sides of the hall (see Chapter 5).

Microphone Checklist

- Amplification is not a substitute for good projection.
- Always ask in advance what type of microphones are being used.
- Make time for a sound check.

- When using any type of radio mic, think carefully about what you will wear so that you can hide the wires and battery pack.
- Headsets must be carefully fitted so that you feel comfortable.
- If you are walking around with a radio mic, make sure you know where the light is and avoid walking in front of the projectors.

CHAPTER 8

Content: Keep It Simple and Direct

In 1946, the then producers of the BBC told me of their "routine." They said: "First you must say what you are going to talk about, secondly you must talk about it, and then you must say what you talked about." That was a prescription for a non-broadcast, if ever there was such a thing. Because I discovered very early on that broadcasting is the control of suspense. No matter what you're talking about—gardening, economics, murder—you're telling a story. Every sentence should lead to the next sentence. If you say a dull sentence, people have a right to switch off.

—Alistair Cooke, Broadcaster of "Letter from America" on BBC Radio for 58 years

There is a huge amount of research on what works and does not work in speeches and verbal presentations. As with any field of human endeavor where there is a wealth of research, there is also a wealth of opinions. Alistair Cooke was presented with one such opinion that is almost conventional wisdom when it comes to presentations. He chose to reject it in favor of a style that he was able to refine over the years and which he made work brilliantly.

You should not rush in to thinking that you know the best and can create a style all of your own without looking first at what we know works well—and does not work. In many business presentations, for instance, the formula Alistair Cooke rejected for his broadcasts works perfectly well.

The really important message here, and which Cooke highlights, is that you are telling a story. Human beings are natural storytellers and also love listening to stories. Too many business presentations are disjoint, rather like listening to a corporate plan being read out aloud. It breaks down into a series of topics, each with its own verbal heading, but with little linkage between one point and the next. They do not lead and provide connections, and therefore do not hold the listener.

To overcome this, you need a good structure with a strong narrative. This will come by having a clear objective for your presentation. This could be:

- To inform
- To motivate
- To persuade
- To debate
- To sell
- To entertain

These are not mutually exclusive. You can, of course, focus tightly on a single objective, perhaps to inform people about a complex or novel topic. Equally, you could set out to motivate people in an entertaining way. Having a clear objective or objectives is the first step to creating a powerful narrative that will engage listeners.

You can also think of a presentation in terms of taking your audience on a journey. This can be most effectively couched in terms of human emotions.

The Emotional Journey

Take your audience

From:	To:
Cynicism	Trust
Apathy	Enthusiasm
Confusion	Understanding
Nervousness	Confidence
Complacency	Concern
Panic	Reassurance
Contempt	Respect
Despair	Hope

Many good sales presentations have this sense of a journey at their heart, but blend that with a very clear message and call to action. They create a sense of need, then present a solution to that need, and finally, persuade the listener to buy into the solution they have presented to them.

The clearer your focus on the objective of a presentation, the easier you will find it to carry your audience with you because the narrative will be more easily sustained throughout the presentation. You may have multiple objectives, which is fine, but you will have to make sure they are all appropriately accommodated in your presentation, and this all goes back to good preparation.

If you do not understand where your audience is starting from in terms of its knowledge and understanding of a subject, or its emotional reaction to it, you will find it very hard to engage them. There is no point in creating a beautifully crafted presentation if it misses the point as far as the audience is concerned. You have to start from where the audience is, not from where you would like them to be.

So, what does all the research mentioned earlier tell us?

One of the most frequent findings is that audiences generally only recall three key concepts from a speech, whether it lasts 10 minutes or two hours. Decide at the outset what your three most important points are. Are they linked in any way? How can you elaborate them in a longer presentation without losing sight of the core three-point structure? Can you also present subsidiary ideas in groups of three?

This does not mean that you construct every presentation in a straight jacket of three concepts, but that when you feel you need to deviate from it—and some topics will demand a different approach—you do so knowing that it is being done for a purpose and to create a specific impact.

Other research says that you should work on no more than one major point every five minutes, up to a maximum of five in half an hour. This is a useful yardstick to apply to longer presentations with a lot of detailed or technical content. Give your audience an opportunity to assimilate one major point before moving onto the next one. The more complex the material, the less familiar the audience may be with the subject, the more care you have to take not to throw too much information at them too quickly.

Research also shows that opinions work better than facts in verbal presentations. This is because opinions engage our emotions, perhaps by challenging views we hold, or reinforcing views. Business presenters often shy away from offering opinions or judgments on the issues they are talking about. This is a missed opportunity. Offer an opinion if at all possible and when appropriate. If you establish yourself as an expert in the minds of an audience, they will expect you to offer your own judgments or at least present sufficient insight to help them on the way to forming their own opinions.

The old maxim so derided by Alistair Cooke—Tell them what you are going to say. Say it. Tell them what you have said—does work so use it, especially if you are making a substantial presentation. It probably is not necessary for a conference or event welcome speech or any short speech with a specific singular purpose. It comes into its own with longer presentations, and you can even afford to put a summary in the middle using a similar formula, reminding people what you have said so far and telling them what you are about to go on to say; always remember that it should be used to sustain a narrative, not to break it up.

You have to learn to start and finish well, or at least with as great a sense of purpose as you can muster.

We have already explored how the speaker's greatest moment of opportunity occurs just after he or she has been introduced and steps to the podium. Use it well. A good introduction is important, and you need to put it across with enthusiasm and commitment, sounding as if you really want to be there (even if you do not).

There is a difficult balance to be struck between creating an effective introduction that gets the audience's attention for the right reasons and going too far with something that is overly contrived or creates expectations that are not going to be fulfilled by what follows.

The best advice is to stick to simple formulas, especially those that you have heard work elsewhere. Great introductions—and great conclusions—do not come easily, and often not at all so knowing what is effective, if simple, is important.

For short presentations, a simple welcome and introduction to the topic or the objective of your presentation will suffice if you cannot come up with something clever and arresting.

With longer presentations you need a well-thought through introduction. The formula A, B, C, and D will help you achieve that.

Attention: get their attention.
Benefits: tell them what they will get out of it.
Credentials: establish a reason for them to have confidence in you.
Direction: make it clear where you are going to take them.

Like all formulas around public speaking, this does not have to be applied rigidly.

You may be able to grab an audience's *attention* with an opening statement: "Today, I am going to show you all how you can become millionaires," and go on to introduce the *benefits*: "I am going to show you how investing in this new fund is easy and cannot fail," and then add your *credentials*: "I put $100 of my own money into this fund and watched it grow to over 100 times that amount," and then show them the *direction* (a little bit of what you are going to tell them): "I will take you through the steps that will help you achieve this success by showing how and when to reinvest and diversify your portfolio."

Alternatively, you could take the same scenario and put your *credentials* first as that might make an arresting, engaging opening getting their *attention* at the same time. You could then set out the *direction* the presentation will take, finishing your introduction by saying "By the end you will have learnt how you can employ these investment strategies to build your wealth," the *benefit* to them.

You may want to tease the audience a little by exposing elements of what you are going to be speaking about, but making it obvious that you are holding something back in the expectation that they will be listening for it later in the presentation. You do not necessarily have to spell out to an audience this is what you are doing as it can be made subtly implicit in what you say and do not say or how you say it.

There are other easy devices that can help create an effective, well-crafted introduction.

Ask the chair or host how you will be introduced: for instance, name and job title or with a full biography. Say thank you for the introduction, and if possible, use it to link into the start of your presentation. If you are particularly keen for the preamble to set up your own introduction by mentioning something specific, then say so: what might seem the obvious thing to mention from your CV to you might not be so obvious to the host.

A personal touch helps get the audience on your side so long as it is not overdone and inappropriate to the occasion. If it can be used to generate empathy with the audience—"I am one of you. I experience the same problems as you do"—then it can work very well.

Topical introductions also work well, as they get the audience thinking the whole presentation is fresh and immediate. If you can relate your presentation to something that is in the news or has recently happened in your business or the market you operate in, it will help get the audience engaged. Again, the caveat here is do not be too contrived. If the link is clear and definitely relevant, then it will work; if it is rather contrived and means people have to stop to think about it, then it will probably not work.

Endings are almost as hard to get right as introductions, so do not leave them to chance. Think about how you are going to finish.

There are a few obvious traps to avoid.

Never say "In conclusion..." or "Finally..." if you do not mean it. By saying anything like that, you instantly set an expectation of speedy passage to the end of your presentation possibly with a neat summary of what you have said, a rounded insight into the subject, or a forceful opinion. People will definitely not expect an extended passage dealing with a new topic or adding a lot of detail that has not been covered earlier. If you suggest you are coming to a close long before you really do, most of the audience will have switched off and will miss or only partially take in your real conclusion.

If you are working with slides, do not get to the last point on your final slide and then suddenly realize you forgot to write an ending. We have all seen speakers surprised that their slides have run out, but have not got a conclusion to fit the end of a presentation. Even a simple "Thank you and I look forward to your questions" is better than nothing.

If you can, try to finish with an opinion, as this invites engagement and emotional responses. This is something audiences definitely respond to, helping them remember what a presentation has been about.

Rhetorical devices can work especially well at the beginning as well as at the end of a speech. For instance, simple repetition of words or phrases can be very effective.

For instance, a speech I scripted for the president of a professional body to its members that had taking pride in what they do as the central theme of its narrative ended like this:

"Be proud—of your profession."

"Be proud—of how you serve your customers."

"Be proud—of the wonderful young people coming through our exams."

"Be proud—of the high standards we all aspire to everyday."

"and Be proud of the fellowship and mutual support our professional body fosters."

It is this sort of device that made many of Britain's wartime Prime Minister Winston Churchill's speeches so effective and memorable. "We shall fight ….," used as a repeated phrase nine times driving toward a forceful concluding phrase that the audience by then believed in: "We shall never surrender" (House of Commons, June 4, 1940). This speech, delivered by the actor Gary Oldman playing Churchill in the film *Darkest Hour*, still brought British cinema audiences to their feet in 2017 (see Figure 8.1).

Figure 8.1 Winston Churchill as Britain's wartime Prime Minister in 1940

Source: Imperial War Museum, London.

Figure 8.2 Martin Luther King Jr. addresses the crowd from the steps of the Lincoln Memorial where he delivered his famous, "I Have a Dream," speech in August 1963

Source: Copyright unattributed.

One of the most famous uses of this rhetorical device was by Martin Luther King in his "I have a dream" speech at the Lincoln Memorial in August 1963. In that, he used the phrase "I have a dream ..." eight times before rising to a dramatic conclusion by repeating the phrase "Let freedom ring ..." nine times. It created one of the most dramatic and memorable speeches in history (see Figure 8.2).

Exhortations to achievement, engagement, or activity make very effective endings so long as they are based on the firm foundations of the preceding content. That has to create a sense of belief among the audience so that, by the end, they believe something is now within their grasp.

The pitch and pace of a conclusion needs careful thought too.

Often, the obvious temptation is to accelerate, raise the volume and sense of excitement for the last few sentences, but it can sometimes be equally effective if you have the right words to slow down, speak a little quieter, and lay a heavy emphasis on the key words. Or you might combine the two techniques: slow down, but raise the volume and punch out the key words. The point is that the style of presentation, as always, matters as much as the content. This is especially true of the most effective, memorable endings.

In between the beginning and end is a middle, and this can be a very difficult area in a longer presentation.

Research shows that, after 20 minutes, an audience's concentration dips dramatically, and unless stimulated, it will only pick up when they know it is near the end. This, then, is the point at which fresh material, video clips, highly controversial topics, and so on should be introduced. Many presenters start with a video, which is almost always a waste at the beginning when you should have the audience's 100 percent attention already: much better to save such stimulating material until the audience's attention is wandering later in a presentation (see Figure 8.3).

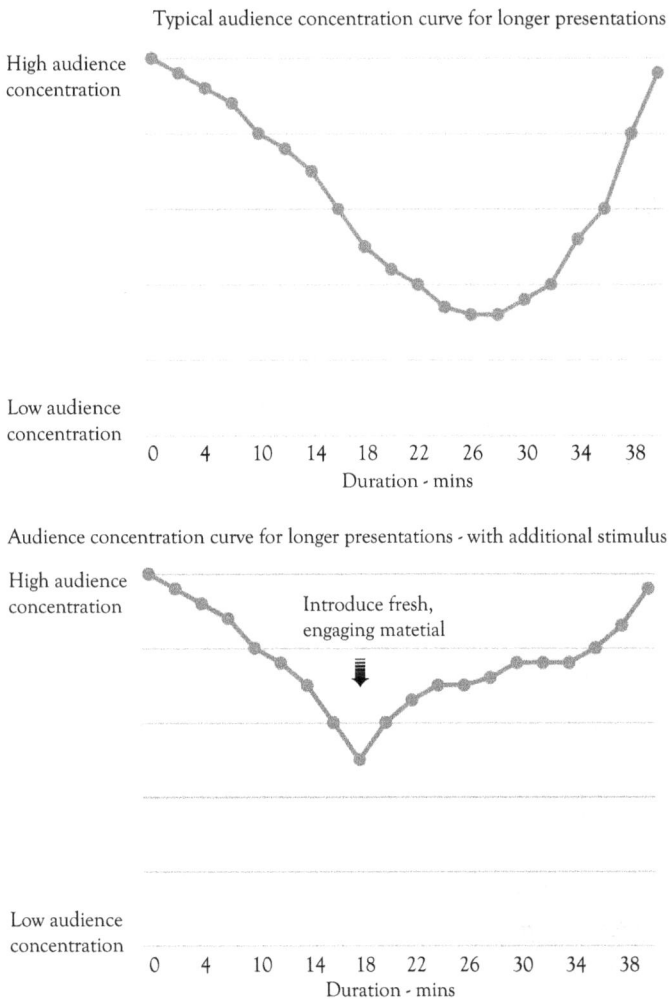

Typical audience concentration curve for longer presentations

Audience concentration curve for longer presentations - with additional stimulus

Figure 8.3 **Audience concentration drops dramatically during longer presentations unless the presenter works hard to lift it**

If you are going to use multimedia always, always check for yourself that it works on the platform and with the equipment you will be using on the stage at the event. Do not take someone's reassurance that what you sent over earlier in the week works fine: ask to see it for yourself on the big screen with you pressing the buttons necessary to get it to run. You do not want to be standing on the stage, holding your breath hoping it works.

Do not expect too much in the way of audience participation, especially at a business event. Throwing out a question and expecting a sea of enthusiastic hands to shoot up is frankly just naïve. Exciting audiences to become part of the presentation is a rare talent, and unless you think you have got it, do not expose yourself to the embarrassment of just a couple of nervous hands going up or, if you are looking for verbal response, being met with a very stony silence.

Many events use apps and other interactive voting technologies to capture audience opinions, and there is more about how to use those in Chapter 13 (Chairing a Conference Session).

As you build the content of your presentation, it is important to keep a firm grip on the narrative by making sure that each point or section logically connects with the next. Think of the techniques of the dramatist or the novelist who works hard to generate suspense, expectation, or inquisitiveness about what is going to happen next. Those tried and trusted techniques of creative writing can be put to work in business presentations.

Avoid too much detail where it is not absolutely essential and be careful with the use of statistics. Preferably in purely verbal presentations, quote statistics as rounded percentages or easy fractions (for instance, "almost half," not 48.56 percent) as these are easier for people to grasp in a verbal presentation. Never use more than two numbers in a sentence unless you are supporting your verbal presentation with slides or handouts when you can afford to go into much more detail (see Chapter 10, Making Slides and AV Work). Where precision in data is essential, this is also where you will need the support of slides or handouts.

Quotes—short and to the point—often work well, as they can be used to provide external authority to what you have just said. They also create an opportunity to adjust the pitch and tone of the presentation slightly. This is not done by mimicking the person who you are quoting, but by using a subtly different tone to indicate that you are quoting someone else's words.

Use jokes sparingly. Humor can be a great aide to a successful presentation, but most of us are not natural stand-up comics. The two key elements to humor in presentations are appropriateness and delivery. Try out any jokes or humorous touches beforehand: ask someone whether they think the humor is right for the audience and the occasion—or even funny—and practice the delivery, especially punch lines. The two tests are always: is it appropriate and can I deliver it. If you cannot be certain that the answer to both questions is a firm *yes*, then leave the jokes out. We have all probably sat through presentations where the speaker thinks they are funny and experienced every emotion from contempt through irritation to sheer embarrassment. Never risk putting yourself in a position to be judged in that way.

Listen to the speakers before you think of the context and subject you are talking about. It is better to keep it straight and risk-free than potentially undermine a good presentation through misjudged humor.

This does not mean that all business presentations need to be deadly serious. On the day, little humorous asides might work well, so learn to judge the mood of your audience. There may be *easy laughs* with particular audiences by mocking certain ideas, organizations, or individuals, and if you are confident, you know where these are to be found and how to press the right buttons to get the desired effect; then, by all means, include them.

The most important ingredient of a good presentation as far as the content is concerned is a strong narrative, sustained consistently throughout the presentation. Add an effective opening and an appropriate—and memorable—ending, and you will be well on the way to crafting an effective speech.

Top Tips for Great Content

- Never forget you are telling a story.
- Build a strong narrative and think of how to create suspense and expectation.
- Be clear on the purpose(s) of your presentation.

- Understand your audience's needs and expectations.
- Work hard on the introduction.
- Work just as hard on the conclusion.
- Take care with using statistics.
- Take even more care with humor: timing, taste, and relevance are the key tests.

CHAPTER 9

To Script or Not to Script?

It usually takes me more than three weeks to prepare a good impromptu speech.

—Mark Twain, American author

In this modern age, we are blessed with any number of options in terms of tools to use help us when we are on our feet in front of an audience. They can also be a curse if not used properly.

There is no simple right or wrong when it comes to using scripts, notes, cue cards, or autocues. Everybody is different, and every event is different. What works for one person at one event will not necessarily work for someone else speaking at the same event. Similarly, what works for you at one event will not always work for you at the next event.

Whether it be full scripts, autocues, prompt cards, notes, or slides, it is always about picking the right tools for the job you have been asked to do.

Full Scripts

Do not be afraid to work from a full script. Many books and courses on speaking advice against this, but scripts can work well in the right circumstances, no more so than when you have a lot of detail to deal with or complex topics to discuss. It is impossible, for instance, to do an awards presentation without a full script with all the names and carefully crafted comments from the judges that have to be delivered perfectly. Autocues are particularly useful if you have a lot of names and job titles to say.

The tendency among speakers and people who offer training in presentation skills to look down on scripts, often dissuading people from using them, can deter inexperienced speakers from venturing out onto the stage. If you feel most comfortable with a scripted presentation, do not let yourself be bullied out of using a script.

One of the greatest speakers of the last century, the British wartime Prime Minister Winston Churchill, used carefully crafted and annotated scripts for all the great speeches he made to Parliament and broadcast on the radio. Indeed, one of the reasons why we have recordings of those speeches he gave in Parliament (which was not broadcast in those days) is that he could go to the radio studio later in the day (or even after the war in some cases) and give precisely the same speech, probably with slightly different intonations but word-for-word the same as Members of Parliament heard earlier (see Figure 9.1).

The full script was Churchill's preferred tool because, when he was first elected to Parliament in 1900, he attempted to live up to the expectations of the day which was that MPs spoke without notes, and certainly without a script. He struggled with this, choosing to write his speeches out and memorize them. The inevitable happened one day when he forgot where he was in his speech and stopped mid-flow, sitting down to jeers from other MPs. After that, he kept his scripts with him for all his speeches.

It is about what works best for you.

Remember, however, that, if you decide to use a script, you are not writing an article or business report to be read out loud. How you present

Figure 9.1 Winston Churchill in 1900, around the time he famously dried up mid-speech in the House of Commons

Source: Connally Collection, Prints and Photographs Division, Library of Congress.

ideas in written communication is rather different from how you deal with the same material in verbal communication where you will need shorter, simpler sentences and need to consider how to deploy rhetorical devices, including emphases and pauses. This means that a script does not have to conform to strict grammatical rules. In particular, you should avoid over-long sentences with too many conjunctions. One idea per sentence is a good rule for a script. Often, it looks wrong on paper, but it will work effectively when spoken. Similarly, with contractions. You will almost always say can't but might write cannot, similarly with doesn't and does not, and so on.

Scrutinize your script for anything that does not work verbally. You have probably all heard speakers refer to an earlier point as being *above* rather than *earlier* or *before*. Key ideas should come at the beginning of sentences, with qualifying phrases following. In writing, we often reverse them. A simple example: "At a meeting in Birmingham last night, the Finance Minister said he would cut taxes" works on the page because you can see the whole sentence, but spoken it would be better as "We will cut taxes, said the Finance Minister at a meeting in Birmingham last night." You must plant the key idea in the listener's mind before qualifying it.

Merely reading a full script can come across as exceedingly dull. It needs practice and rehearsal to bring it alive. It can be useful to think of using a script as similar to reading a story to a group of young children. There are two objectives in that case. The first is you want to send them to sleep in which case reading it in a dull, flat monotone will usually do the trick. The second is you want to excite and energize them. In that case, you have to work to bring the story alive, stressing the exciting words, using different tones and voices for the various characters, and all the way through varying the pace and the pitch. That is the approach that needs to be taken to making a speech from a script.

You will need to rehearse thoroughly with a clear focus on how to make it sound animated and spontaneous. Make a point of getting very familiar with some passages so that you will feel confident enough to look up and engage the audience when you deliver it.

When you read your script out loud, pay attention to awkward words, clumsy phrases, and sentences that work perfectly well on paper, but which you are struggling to bring alive orally. If the initial draft of the script has been prepared for you by someone else, you will need to work particularly hard at this. Even if they are a top-class script writer, they are not you, and even more importantly, they do not have to stand up in front of an audience and make it work.

In addition to having all the words in front of you, with a full script, you can also write all the cues for slides and gestures and even highlight the passages and phrases you want to emphasize. Another big advantage is that you can time your presentation carefully.

Do not staple your pages together as turning them over will look awkward when you are up on the stage and might cause a lot of rustling noise that will be picked up by the microphones. You should slide the pages across each other as you move from one to the next. The pages should be clearly numbered, and if you are worried about them getting out of order, use a tie in one corner rather than a staple, as this will make the pages much easier to turn over or discreetly detach from each other as you are speaking. Always end a page with a complete sentence. If you break a sentence across two pages, you will make a potential trap for yourself as you might stumble over it as you turn the pages and move your eyes quickly from the bottom of one page to the top of the next.

Keep the script with you. Even if you are the first or only speaker up, do not be tempted to leave it on the lectern: there are too many tales of some over enthusiastic production assistant tidying up the stage and removing all the papers just before the start. Imagine walking up to the lectern expecting find your script neatly placed in front of you only to find that it has vanished.

Using an Autocue

You can have your script displayed on an autocue (sometimes called a teleprompter). They are widely used because they can be very effective for longer presentations that need to be carefully scripted. You do need to be familiar with how they work.

If you do have the opportunity to use an autocue, always make sure you have a chance to rehearse so that you are happy with the height and angle of the screens and the speed at which the text comes up. Check beforehand whether you will have one or two screens: two is hugely preferable because the setup will make you move your head from one screen to the other. If you do have two screens placed on either side of the rostrum, do remember to look at the section of the audience straight in front of you from time to time. Do not become totally dependent on reading every word from the autocue. If you have just a single screen placed straight in front of you, the need to take your eyes away from the screen from time to time becomes even more important. Always think of how you can use your eyes to engage an audience and *work the room* (see Chapter 5).

You should ask to go through the whole thing so that you can check that all of the text has been correctly loaded. Look out for strange word or line breaks and get them adjusted so that you do not hesitate as your eyes scan the screen for the rest of a word or sentence.

Autocues can be automated or might have an operator. In the case of an automated autocue, make sure that the speed setting is the one you are very comfortable with. If you want to put some pauses in between the sections, ensure that sufficient space is left to take account of them.

It is much better to have manually operated autocues. Operators will follow your speed. This means that, if you speed up for a passage, then the autocue will run faster. Be careful not to fall into the trap of then treating this as a new default speed. If you want to pause or slowdown, that will be fine as the operator will follow you.

Make sure you have a written version of your speech to hand—technology does fail occasionally.

Autocues really come into their own when you have presentations that have a lot of names or other detailed information in them. Awards ceremonies are an obvious case because you will have long lists of names, companies, and products, but will really need to keep the maximum engagement with the audience, so a head buried in a script is to be avoided (see Chapter 14 Awards Ceremonies).

Write any names phonetically where there is any doubt about how they might be pronounced: you are the only person who can see it and it is important that you get these right. If there are long numbers and your script is on an autocue, write them out in words as a six figure number might only be six characters as a numeral, but it will consist of many syllables when spoken and will race by if not written out as words.

Cue Cards Often Work Well

Using cue cards or prompt cards works very well for most presentations, especially if you are confident with the material and subject. For many business speakers, they are the default option. You should still rehearse the whole presentation, however. You may want to write out a verbatim particularly important or telling points and phrases, especially opening and closing remarks.

If you do use cue cards, do not let your presentation become unstructured or allow it to over-run. This can be easy trap to fall into once you warm to your subject and audience and stray from your original content plan. You can guard against the danger of this getting out of hand by putting approximate timings against the sections of your presentation.

Always remember to number your cards clearly or tag them together. Again, keep them with you at all times.

If your presentation is supported by slides, do not be lazy and use the slides alone as your prompt, as you will often end up reading out what people can see on the slide. Everything you say should complement, not merely repeat, what is on the screen. There is more advice in Chapter 10 Making Slides and AV Work for the Audience.

Unscripted, or Is It?

You could go completely unscripted, but beware.

At the opposite extreme from a fully scripted presentation is an unscripted one. Some speakers who use this approach will have virtually memorized what they are going to say or just be so familiar with the subject that they can talk confidently without the help of a script or notes. It does work extremely well in terms of audience engagement, but is definitely one for the very experienced. If you do try this, always have some notes to hand just in case you feel your presentation is losing its way or you are in danger of forgetting some key piece of information.

Often, the greatest risk with a genuinely unscripted presentation is that you lose control of the time. If you have any doubt about your ability to keep to time or avoid rambling or deviating too much from the core narrative, practice the presentation and record it. If nothing else, that will help you judge where the points at which you might be in danger of going off on a tangent might be.

Timekeeping

Whatever approach you take, do not out-stay your welcome.

Ideally, you should aim to finish a little under your allotted time. It is always far better to leave people thinking they could have listened to you for a while longer, rather than have them sitting there wondering when you are going to stop.

If you do find yourself running short of time, drop a whole section rather than rush (and potentially garble) the rest of your presentation. If you are using slides you may just have to say that you will skip over a few as you are running out of time. Never put yourself in the position of being asked by the chair or host to wind-up or stop.

To ensure this does not happen, you have to be the master of your own time. Make sure you can see a watch, clock, or timer. If there is not a clock on the rostrum, take your watch off and use that—do not keep it on your wrist as it will be very obvious to the audience that you are worried about the time as you keep glancing down at it.

The organizers might have their own timekeeping systems. At some events, there will be a system of *traffic lights* on the rostrum with green, amber, and red lights. Make sure you know how these are going to be used, especially how long you have got left once the amber light comes on and whether the red light signals that the chair is likely to intervene very quickly.

An alternative might be a countdown timer on the rostrum or mounted on the floor in your sightline. Often, these also use green, amber, and red to make it obvious how long you have left.

If organizers have gone to the trouble of setting up timers to help you, it means they are concerned to run their event to schedule: you should respect that.

Question and Answer Sessions

You may be expected to participate in a question and answer session following your presentation or participate in a panel with other speakers. Check in advance how this will be run so that you are not caught out by being asked to take questions at the end of your speech or join a panel.

Whether the questions are just aimed at you or you are part of a panel, this should not be treated as an opportunity to make another speech. You should keep answers short and to the point. If you are on a panel, try to bounce the issue back to one of the other speakers so that some sort of debate or dialogue can be maintained. Above all, answer the question. It is often helpful to jot down the key points as the question(s) is being put, especially if it is not well structured or rolls several questions up together.

Whenever possible, make eye contact with the questioner as you begin your answer. This should be possible even in relatively large halls. It will make them feel you care about their contribution and make people more likely to engage with you.

Scripting Checklist

- Pick the right tools for the job.
- Full scripts need to be rehearsed to bring them alive.
- If using notes or speaking without them, make sure you stick to the narrative.
- Autocues can be very useful, but need proper practise.
- Care about timekeeping: do not out-stay your welcome.

CHAPTER 10

Making Slides and AV Work for the Audience

People do not live by pie charts alone—or by bar graphs, or three inch statistical appendices to 300 page reports. People live, reason and are moved by symbols and stories.
>   —Tom Peters, author of "In Search of Excellence"

One of the biggest problems facing presenters today is to know how to use visual aids, especially slides. Everyone will have heard the criticism of having to sit through a presentation that was *death by PowerPoint*. There is no doubt that slides are over-used. Speakers use them when they do not need them. They have become a crutch they feel they cannot do without. On other occasions, people use far too many or clutter them up with excessive amounts of detail.

The best thing you can say about most options for audio-visual support during a presentation is that, at least, they are usually reliable nowadays, although you should not take risks by turning up with a PowerPoint presentation on a memory stick and hope it will work. Send it over in advance, and when you arrive, ask to check that it looks the same and builds the same way as when it left you and that any video content or websites load correctly.

PowerPoint seems to have become the standard for professional conference presentations. Overhead projected slides still have their uses in some environments, especially if you have diagrams, tables, and so on that work best if revealed gradually, or if you want to invite contributions from the audience to add to them as might be the case in a workshop-style event. This can also be done on sophisticated touch screens as well, a technology that has developed rapidly in the last few years. Pick whatever you think will work best, having checked with the organizers what their expectation is and what they can provide.

With PowerPoint or similar programs, you need to think carefully about how you use them to ensure they benefit your audience.

What you put on slides should complement what you are saying. Do not just put your cue card bullet points up and read them out as people will read them for themselves and stop listening to you.

Do not make them too cluttered. This is a difficult one to call sometimes as it is as much a function of the size of screen and proximity of the audience as what you put on the slide. It comes down to early preparation to avoid creating problems by not matching the content of your slides to the size of screen and distribution of the audience (see Figure 10.1).

PowerPoint undoubtedly comes into its own when you have complex data, graphs, or concepts to present. Financial information, in particular, often needs the precision that only a slide presentation can deliver. There are a lot of factors to consider in order to create a presentation that is going to engage and inform your audience.

One key to getting it right is to keep thinking as you create the slides just how they are going to look to the audience in the venue and with the screen size and resolution you will have available. What works on a desktop screen with high resolution might appear completely unreadable to someone sitting near the back of a hall where the screen is too small and bright sunlight is streaming through the windows. They will stop listening to you because they cannot read what it is that you are taking the trouble of explaining.

If you are using PowerPoint for complex presentations, you should learn how to use all of its many features effectively. There are plenty of online courses and guides that can quickly enhance your knowledge and skills. There is no excuse for putting up bland, boring, badly laid-out slides, lacking visual interest.

Some of the most common faults are about putting too much onto a single slide. Sometimes, this can be solved by building the information step-by-step, rather than slapping it up all at once. Take a graph with various lines showing trends that you want to explain to the audience how they contrast or interact. Put them up all at once, and at a distance, it might look confused, the colors might be fainter than on your desktop screen, and the key points be lost on many in the audience. Add a line at a time and people will see them all more clearly and quickly gain a clearer

The Insurance Voice

- What voice?
- One or many? Division is fatal
- Leave it to the professionals
- Mixed record over the last 30 years
- Consistency and long term view is key

Old journalism

- In the past journalists would:

Research

Write

Publish

&
Repeat....

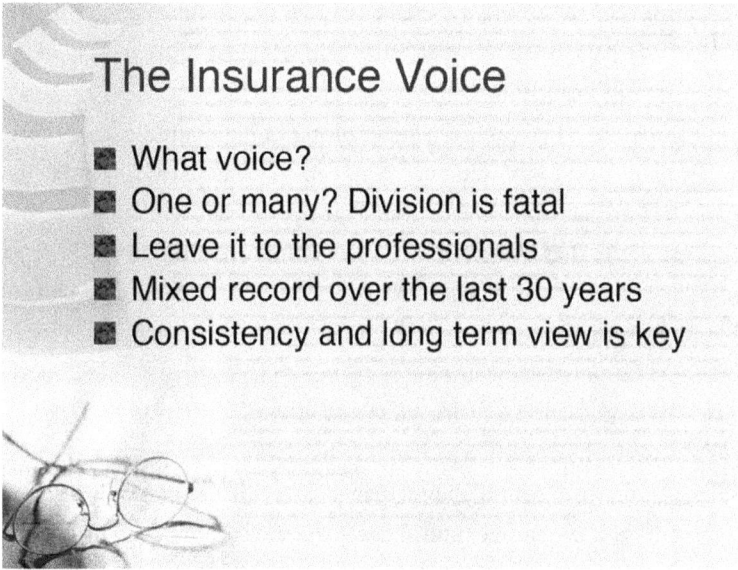

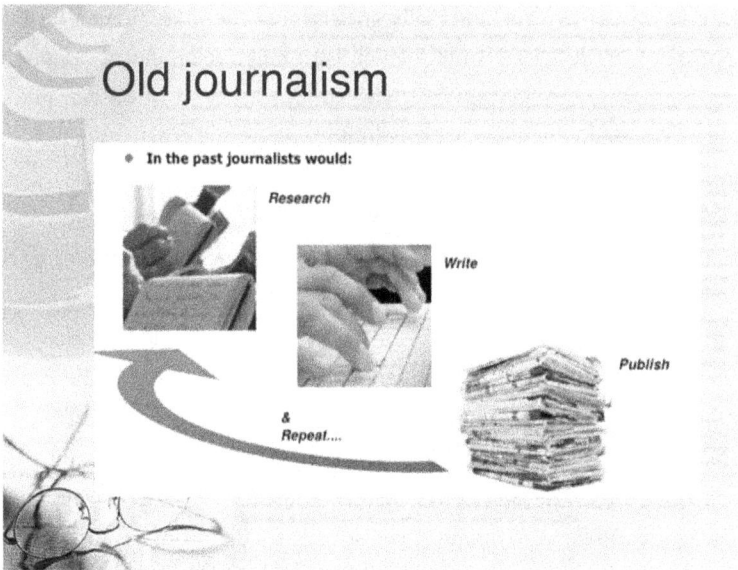

Figure 10.1 Keep slides simple and use graphics effectively

Source: Credit: David Worsfold

understanding of the key points. This will also help people who have any form of colorblindness, a more common condition than many of us imagine. In the United States, one in 76 people suffers from some form of colorblindness,[1] so in an audience of 100 people, the chances are that at least one person will be struggling to distinguish the carefully chosen colors of your beautifully constructed chart.

Alternatively, you can use a laser pointer to highlight the key points as you explain them to the audience. This can come across as slightly schoolmasterly, but that can still work with the appropriate audience.

Even slides that contain a list of key points are often better built one point at a time. If you put too many words up at once, people will stop listening to you in order to read the slide, and also, you may have revealed too much about what you are going to say next, giving them another reason to switch off from what you are saying.

You want the audience to look at you, rather than get fixated by the slides. Audience research shows that people will divide their attention better between the speaker and slides if the slides are not too bright. This is a tricky balance to get right. Avoiding overly bright (white) slides might seem very obvious, but it actually goes against the most frequently used approaches to designing slides, which is to make them clean, often with very plain white backgrounds. If you are putting a lot of data or graphs relying on easily distinguishable colored lines or bars, then a white background is the most obvious and safest option.

If the slide largely contains words, bold symbols, or simple charts, then it is better to consider using a muted color—pastels are good—as the background with simple, clear lettering.

As mentioned in Chapter 8 on content, using audio or video clips can really help lift a longer presentation, especially around the crucial 20-minute mark when people's attention begins to wane. You must check what formats the organizers can cope with and whether they want them embedded in a slide show or run as separate clips. Always, always check they work and be very careful if you stream a video from a website as the strength of the connection or the Wi-Fi signal may vary between testing it and using it live.

While you are checking that everything works as you intend it to, make sure you know how to change the slides and how to go back if you need to. If you want to walk around while using the slides, you will

---

[1] US Census Bureau, Population Estimates, 2004.

need a hand-held control, so make sure you notify the organizers of this requirement in advance.

Speaking to the slides is not quite as easy as most people imagine. Yes, you have the narrative of your presentation embedded in a slide show that you are sharing with the whole audience. It ensures you have a sound structure and a clear direction. Those are definitely benefits.

Too often people make the mistake of speaking to their slides and not to the audience. It is very tempting to turn away from the rostrum and the audience to look at the screen when you are speaking to a slide presentation. Some people do it because they are seeking a reassurance that the slides are appearing correctly. Often, speakers are not even particularly aware that they are doing this. It very quickly disengages you from the audience. Almost always, nowadays, speakers are able to see their slides as they change and build on a screen positioned on the lectern or on the floor in front of them. Often, these can be set, so you can see both the current slide and the next one in the pack. You must learn to trust these screens and remain facing the audience as you explain what is on a slide.

A secondary problem if you turn to look at the screen and keep talking while you do so is that you will be turning away from the microphones, unless you are using a lapel mic or headset. This will mean your voice will fade away and then return loudly as you switch between looking at the audience and the screen behind you. That is not an effect that will enhance the audience's listening experience and is another compelling reason as to why you need to discipline yourself to stay facing the audience.

If you use a laser pointer, this will increase the temptation to turn away from the audience and microphones, so work hard on ensuring that you keep this to the minimum.

However you create, design, and handle slides; above all, remember that you are still talking to an audience. Having a good slide presentation does not let you off getting all the other aspects of presentational technique right.

AV and PowerPoint Checklist

- Choose when and how to use slides carefully.
- Make sure the slides and content on them is suitably presented for the venue.

- Double-check that they change and build properly.
- Learn how to present complex data so that it is easily intelligible.
- Never just read out what is on your slides.
- Make sure you stay facing the audience, not the screen.

CHAPTER 11

Hosting and Facilitating Events

Let our advance worrying become advance thinking and planning.
—Winston Churchill, British politician and
wartime prime minister

Good presenters are frequently asked to combine a speech with hosting a panel session at a conference or to chair a whole conference session or to act as a facilitator for a roundtable discussion. This requires the effective deployment of many of the techniques discussed in the earlier chapters, but now combined with people management skills.

Let us step back and consider what is a chair or facilitator there for?

Traditionally, the role of a chair was fairly passive, just calling people to speak at meetings and conferences as they indicated, sticking to a timetable, and if necessary, keeping order.

Nowadays, a chair is expected to be very proactive in prompting and sustaining the discussion. Approach any event you are asked to facilitate, no matter how small, with the expectation that it will be up to you to make sure discussions happen and that everyone gets a chance to make a contribution.

The modern chair is a facilitator, actively managing the discussion and stimulating debate. What that actually means depends on many factors: the format of the event, the subject, the nature of the audience (if there is one), and the quality and co-operation of the key participants.

Among the common definitions of facilitate are *to make easy* or *ease a process*. What a facilitator does is plan, guide, and manage an event to ensure that its objectives are met effectively with good participation from everyone who is involved (see Figure 11.1).

Figure 11.1 The author chairing a panel session: knowing the speakers and engaging with the audience is key to being a successful facilitator

Source: Credit: Steve Dazko/Infopro Digital

The mantra of preparation, preparation, preparation applies just as much to this role as it does to that of speaker.

Never underestimate the value of proper preparation. Even what can appear to be the most spontaneous of events is often carefully rehearsed and runs within a carefully prepared framework. You must have a clear idea of the purpose of the event if you are to guide it to a successful conclusion. It will make you a little more relaxed as you will feel more in control and will eliminate the scope for too many nasty surprises. Preparation covers several areas as we have seen when learning how to prepare for our own presentations in Chapter 2.

The Five Points of Proper Preparation

1. Know your subject

Make sure you know as much as possible about the key headline issues in the topic being discussed or debated. Focus particularly on the controversial issues because this is probably what everyone will want to talk about, but often be frightened to raise. Pre-event research among the potential audience is a useful way of making sure you are asking the questions the audience wants to hear answered, and therefore keeping them engaged. This is very easy to do nowadays with e-mail bulletins, websites, and apps to support events.

2. **Know your speakers, panelists, or guests**

Ensure you know as much as possible about the people you are in control of. Check whether they have had much to say recently about the topics you have identified as key issues.

If it is a panel session at a conference and you want to fire some potentially controversial questions at them, warn them beforehand. Your job is not usually to look clever by catching people out, but to ensure that information is imparted to the audience or shared among the guests.

Similarly, if you think that one of the speakers has access to some detailed information that you want to discuss, prime them beforehand; this might take a telephone call or e-mail exchange a few days before.

If you think the topic(s) is particularly complex or controversial or the panelists potentially difficult, either because of lack of experience or because they have a reputation for dominating discussions, you should also consider contacting them in advance to let them know what is expected and tell them how you will run the session. Sometimes, it might be necessary to arrange a conference call so that you can be sure everyone buys into the format and understands what is expected of them.

3. **Know your audience**

Who is in the audience? What are the key issues from their perspective? They may be expecting you to ask all the questions, so make sure you know what matters to them. Obviously, for some events, such as a webcast, the facilitator is clearly expected to put the questions to the panelists, albeit sometimes incorporating questions submitted by e-mail, social media, or via an app by the listening external audience. These tools are commonly used at face-to-face events nowadays as well.

4. **Know your venue**

You want to feel as comfortable as possible in a stressful situation, and knowing the venue certainly helps. If you can visit it beforehand, then do so, whether it is just a private room in a restaurant or a large conference hall, although the latter without the stage is not always that useful. If it is a webcast, try to visit the studio beforehand, observe a webcast in action, and familiarize yourself with the technology and controls.

There are plenty of things you should look out for in a venue and these are explored next, but the main things you should think about for any live event are: What will work for me? Where will I sit? Will I stand up to speak? If so, where will I speak from? How do I keep control of the time? Can all of the participants see me?

5. Know your technology

Make sure you know what technology is involved and available and whether it is expected that you will use it. This covers sound, lighting, visual aids, and any audience interaction tools. On the whole, if you are chairing or introducing a conference and there are slides, a simple title slide is enough. You should be familiar with the presentations that will be on screen for any session you are managing.

There may be facilities for live questions to be submitted electronically or via social media, so you need to check this out beforehand and feel confident that you can use it effectively. Often, this will involve taking the audience through how to use the technology at the beginning of the event, so you will have to prepare an explanation, ensuring it gives people time to log on, find the event, and work out how to vote. Too often, presenters rush into the early questions before everyone in the audience has even logged on.

There are many different roles a good facilitator can play. Sometimes, this is clear from the outset, but that is not always the case. You may have been asked because you have an obvious aptitude for guiding roundtables or panel discussions, or you may have been asked because you have the knowledge and expertise to be able to pose the right the questions to an expert group. A key factor to pin down before you start is whether you are expected to be neutral or contribute your own views in order to stimulate the discussion.

Whatever type of facilitator you have been asked to be, in order to be effective, you must know when to take a leadership role and when to be neutral and take a back seat. This is a difficult balance to strike. The key to being a successful facilitator is to plan the session or event thoroughly and remain focused on the overall objective, rather than get drawn in too deeply with specific content and opinions.

So, how do you apply those five basic rules of proper preparation to different types of event? The next two chapters look at two of the most frequent examples of the sort of events effective presenters are likely to be asked to facilitate: roundtables and panel debates.

There are, of course, many other types of activities that require facilitating, such as ideas sharing and generation, get-to-know you events, corporate away days, and so forth. These require special skills that are not necessarily natural or relevant to the public speaker and are beyond the scope of this book.

Basic Rules of Effective Facilitation

- Be clear on what role are you expected to play.
- Facilitation is a highly proactive role, so be well prepared to lead, but know when to step back.
- Proper preparation is essential.
- Stay focused on the overall objective of the discussion.

CHAPTER 12

Making Roundtables Work

A wise man speaks because he has something to say, a fool speaks because he has to say something.

—Plato, early Greek philosopher

On paper, roundtable debates and discussions should be the easiest, although sometimes they can still be hard work for the chair, especially if they are conducted over a meal, a popular format in some business circles. The main problem you can face with this format is sustaining the discussion through three courses and coffee. If it dries up after the main course, you can hardly say: "Okay, we seem to have exhausted that subject, let's pack up and go home!" It will fall to you to keep it going. This is where thorough preparation is essential.

If it is a long roundtable—with or without a meal—it is worth thinking about how the key tasks can be divided up so that they do not all fall on one person; for instance, introduction, chairing, summing up. You can also create a structured agenda for the discussion, which is shared with the participants, so they know the sequence of topics, timings, and so on (see Figure 12.1).

How are the five rules of preparation applied to roundtables?

1. Know your subject

Knowledge of the subject is very important as a roundtable is likely to be a fairly detailed, in-depth discussion among experts. As a facilitator, you do not have to be an expert yourself, but you will need a clear grasp of what matters to the participants, where the real issues are, any points of controversy, and be equipped to steer the discussion into the areas of genuine interest, avoiding being dragged into lengthy detours around tangential topics.

Figure 12.1 Roundtables take many forms and the tables come in all shapes and sizes

Source: Credit: Infopro Digital

2. Know the participants

Who are the people sitting around you? Knowing the participants is absolutely key for a roundtable, as you will have to proactively manage them to get the best out of them and ensure the roundtable achieves its objectives. Find what they, their companies, or organizations have had to say on the topic(s) under discussion. Why are they there and what is their relationship to the subject matter and the issues? You can use that material to draw people into the discussion as it progresses and ensure everyone gets an adequate opportunity to contribute.

You should also make sure you know where people are sitting. If possible, you should have a table plan in front of you and all the guests should have two-sided place-cards so that everyone can see who is sitting where. If it is one of your own company's events, you should be in control of this anyway, but even if you are doing this for someone else, you should still ask for these things. Sometimes, it will not be possible or appropriate to do this, as people will just be invited to sit where they want. In this case, you should still have a guest list and a blank table plan so that you can fill in where people are as they introduce themselves. You will be amazed how the mind

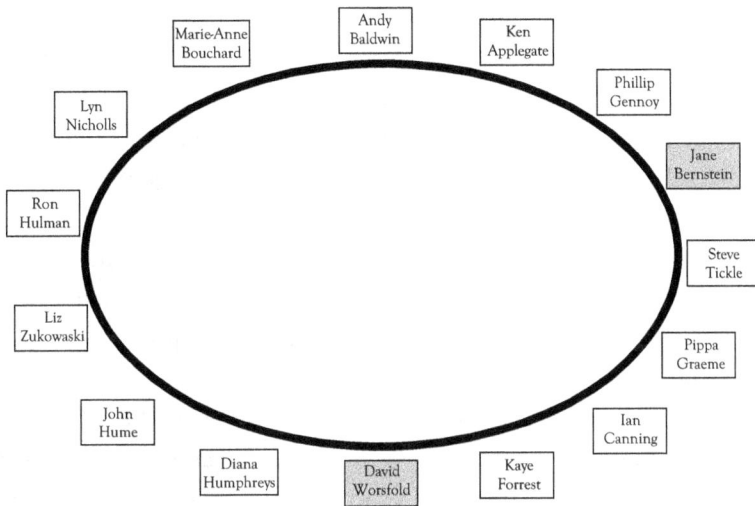

Figure 12.2 Have clear table plan so you know who is sitting where

Source: Credit: David Worsfold

can go blank at the crucial moment and you forget who is who just as you want to bring someone into the discussion (see Figure 12.2).

3. **Know your audience**

   There might not be an audience in the room, but if the roundtable is being used to generate a report or is being recorded for later distribution, you must keep in mind what interests the potential readers and listeners and make sure that those topics are addressed. You need to consider what expectations the users who download or view it might have, and ensure you bear those in mind as the discussion develops. If it is being recorded, you will need to remind the participants not to forget the external audience.

4. **Know your venue**

   Often, people think understanding how the venue might impact the event is not too important for a roundtable, but it is.

   If possible, avoid long, narrow, oblong tables, as it is hard to see people at the ends of the long sides, and you do not really want to sit at the head of the table as this potentially detaches some people from the discussion. Oval, square, or round tables are best.

The facilitator needs to make sure they can see everyone from where they will be sitting. This is not always as easy as you might think as the venue or organizers may have put large table decorations, candelabras, or flower arrangements in your sightlines, especially if it is held in a private dining room or a restaurant. You should get them moved if you think they might hide a participant from you (also, remember that photographers will not like them either).

If you can, make sure you have a little more space around your place so that you can put some notes and a table plan down where you can easily refer to them.

When the roundtable is combined with breakfast, lunch, or dinner, make sure that the catering staff knows when you want the food served. Some restaurants are very reluctant to serve while people are speaking and will need to be told that is what you expect if you want it to run continuously. Alternatively, short pauses as food is served can be used to break up the discussion into different topics.

5. Know your technology

This is perhaps a lesser consideration for a roundtable unless it is being recorded. If it is being recorded, tell people and point out where the microphones or video cameras are. You might also need to check the lighting levels with the photographer and make sure they can move around the table with ease, so they do not become a distraction.

Quietly authoritative, proactive management is the key to facilitating a successful roundtable, and you need to set the right tone for this from the very beginning.

When introducing a round table welcome everybody on behalf of the host and any sponsors and remind them of the subject and what the objectives are, for instance, producing a report, a podcast, or just thrashing out the issues among a group of influential people.

If relevant, explain that it is for reporting and will be *on the record* unless someone specifically requests otherwise before saying something. Be very careful if people start talking about *Chatham House Rules*, as they usually do not understand them, and it can be the source of confusion—and even irritation—after the event. The Chatham House Rule—and there is only one rule—is that the discussion is attributable (with none of the participants identified), but not off the record.[1]

As an example, this means that someone could write a report (or a news story if there is a journalist present) saying "At a discussion in the city last night, top executives were very critical of the regulator's proposals on key issues." It could then go on to paraphrase what was said, even directly quoting people if that does not risk identifying them. Most people who attend an event they believe is being held under *Chatham House Rules* would be horrified to see such a report. Be clear on what will be produced after the event.

If it is meant to be an *on-the-record* event with a report or recording produced later, it is best to discourage people from chipping in with *off-the-record* comments. It can be very hard afterward to work out when the comments went off the record and when they came back on the record. In very exceptional circumstances, an off-the-record contribution might add some valuable information or insight to a discussion. In this case, ask the person to clarify that they are going off the record before they make the comment and to confirm when they are coming back on the record.

Of course, if the whole discussion is meant to be confidential, these considerations are not a concern.

So, having clarified these key points, how do you get a discussion going?

Tell the participants how you intend running the discussion, for instance, there could be a prepared introduction from one of the guests or yourself, or you could pose specific questions from time-to-time. This really should have been communicated to them in advance, but you still need to remind people at the event.

Let them know how long the discussion will last and what time you intend winding it up and stick to that; otherwise, you will have people drifting away or start checking phones and e-mails under the table.

Give them a few pointers for the discussion or hand over to someone who has been asked to prepare a short introduction.

---

[1] https://www.chathamhouse.org/chatham-house-rule (accessed on September 12, 2018).

One of the logistical challenges everyone who hosts a roundtable event has to address is whether participants should be asked to introduce themselves.

If it is a group that clearly already knows each other well, it is usually possible to avoid going round the table and getting everyone to introduce themselves. It is time consuming and boring if they already know each other. Use your table plan, and if you have them, the two-sided place-cards to bring people in to the discussion by name (together with position, department, or company the first time).

If it is a group of people less likely to know each other or you have chosen to let people sit where they like, a quick *round-the-table* introduction will be needed. You should start it off yourself by keeping it short and to the point, thereby setting the style for everyone else to follow. It is one of those unfortunate rules that, if you pass the responsibility of doing the first introduction to someone else, they will make it long-winded, setting a precedent for everyone else to follow. If they really have done or said something or have been involved in something recently that needs explaining, encourage them to introduce that when they join in the discussion.

Once you have got the introductions out of the way, you need to keep the momentum going by moving into the discussion, perhaps by asking a question. It is often useful to have someone prepared to answer first or set the scene, so another voice is quickly introduced into the discussion.

It is obviously an essential requirement of a roundtable to ensure everyone has the opportunity to have their say. If you can *meet and greet* each guest as they arrive for the event, try to ask them what made them come, what the key issue is for them, or what they hope to get out of the roundtable; it could be useful later if you need a handle to bring someone in. The background work prior to the event should also help, as you will know which guests and companies have recently had something to say on the topics under discussion.

You might find you have one or two dominant speakers. This is where using the knowledge of what others want to talk about or may have a clear view on comes in very useful. Do not be afraid to interrupt and say, for example, "That's a great point. Let's get some reaction from X whose company has just done the opposite" (or whatever).

Alternatively, you may find yourself dealing with Plato's fool. Coping with a dominant speaker or a participant who seems to be determined to pursue their own, quite often only loosely related, agenda is the toughest part of being a roundtable host. It is not something that can be ducked, as other participants will not thank you for letting one person run away with the discussion. Also, the material for any write-up or podcast afterward will be very skewed toward one person's viewpoint.

You need to develop a range of verbal and visual tools to deal with these situations and have the confidence to use them. Body language is especially important in the close-quarters environment of a roundtable. Think of it as giving yourself some gears you can go through in order to maintain or wrest back control.

Sit back a little in your seat as much as possible. This gives you the option of leaning forward onto the table as a signal that you are going to intervene. If someone has indicated they want to come into the discussion, but someone else is speaking for too long, make it clear to everyone around the table that you have acknowledged the request to come in.

If the person who is speaking still does not take the hint, lean toward them and look at them, trying to catch their eye. There will be occasions when this fails too, in which case, direct intervention is the only option. By using phrases such as "That's a great point, let's get a response to that," you can intervene firmly and decisively and ensure you quickly get another participant talking without, hopefully, causing undue offence to the person you have had to shut up. If you do this, you must succeed as a half-hearted, failed attempt to intervene will mean you lose control of the debate.

Adding some additional body language can also help, such as holding up your hand as a *stop* signal.

Sometimes, a facilitator faces the opposite problem: the quiet or reluctant participant. This can happen for all sorts of reasons, ranging from natural shyness, through being intimidated by having more senior people round the table to being a last-minute substitute for another participant. This is where good prior knowledge of the people as well as the issues helps enormously.

A pause is often a good chance to move the discussion on by bringing in someone who has been quiet up until then. Once invited, most people will respond quickly and become active participants.

On other occasions, you may need to do more to create a platform for the quiet participant to make their contribution(s) by cuing them up with a short introduction such as "I know your company has done something interesting in this area recently. How has that worked out?" Usually, once they have spoken once, they will feel more inclined to intervene later on, but you may have to return to them in a similar way in order to keep them involved.

The most difficult types of interventions are those when conflict and disagreement start getting out of hand. Usually, you want a lively and robust debate, but you have to keep control of it.

It should go without saying that a good chair should step in and mediate immediately if there are obvious personal attacks. This is where thinking in terms of having a range of gears you can go through is also very useful. Effective facilitators look for the least intrusive intervention first, so reminding everyone of the overall objectives, and if relevant, the external audience's expectations is often a good place to start if. Phrases such as "It will be best if we stick to the issues, rather than personalise them" or "I know there are strong views around the table, but let's ensure we address them constructively" are usually enough to do the trick.

If they do not work, then you have little option other than to make clear that personal attacks cannot be tolerated. The dangers you face at a roundtable are that if other participants feel they are being attacked they might retaliate in kind, in which case, the whole event is significantly devalued, or they may just decide to leave. Whatever the issue, you cannot allow bad behavior to continue, so be prepared to take the steps necessary to stop attacks.

Every discussion needs to be steered toward a conclusion, hopefully by noting that you have achieved the objectives agreed at the outset. It must also finish on time. Making sure you can see a clock or watch is, therefore, important.

Always aim to wind-up in good time so that people have a chance to chat among themselves or leave if they have only allowed the time it was advertised the event was going to last. It is often helpful if you or someone else (pre-warned of course) can briefly summarize the discussion. This can help the participants leave feeling they have achieved something.

Whichever option you choose—whether you sum up or someone else does—remember to finish by thanking everyone for their participation, thank the host or sponsor(s), and remind people of the post-event elements, such as publication of a report or production of a podcast or video.

Roundtable Key Points

- Be clear on your role: neutral facilitator or proactive questioner.
- Research the participants so that you know why they are there.
- Be clear on the objectives and how it will be run.
- Set the right tone from the outset.
- Think in terms of having visual and oral *gears* you can go through when intervention is necessary.

CHAPTER 13

Chairing Conference Sessions and Panel Debates

Anything I've ever done that ultimately was worthwhile—initially scared me to death.
  —Betty Bender, president of the U.S. Library Administration and Management Association (LAMA) from 1986 to 1989

The prospect of chairing a conference session or a panel debate at a conference might appear more daunting than a roundtable, not least because there will be a live audience in front of you and often a panel of high-powered experts to manage. Again, it can be made much less stressful and scary through applying the five rules of proper preparation.

1. **Know your subject**
   A thorough knowledge of the topics likely to be discussed is essential if you are to handle the participants and the questions with confidence, ensuring that the issues are addressed—and not ducked—by the participants. If it is a session involving presentations, try to look at the slides or papers of the speakers you will be introducing ahead of the day and draft some questions based on them. You may find it helpful to call the speakers in advance to discuss the content of their presentations or arrange a conference call if you have two or three speakers covering similar topics.

2. **Know your speakers**
   You should have biographies of the speakers, which should help. Do not read them out as the delegates should have them in their packs or in an online app. Introduce them by name, job title, company, and a short sentence about what they have done recently or a fact that

underlines their qualification to be talking on the subject. An ideal introduction should excite the audience so that they believe in the speaker before they start. What they do once you have set them up is down to them. If in any doubt about pronunciation of people's or company names, check in advance. Write down any tricky names phonetically if you are in any doubt about your ability to pronounce them correctly.

3. Know your audience

If you are expected to involve the audience—and that is most likely to be the case—it is absolutely essential that you know something about them. What type of people have you got sitting in front of you? What is their interest in the subject and what are their likely concerns? What issues do they have with the speakers or their organizations? Will they have raised the right issues? You need to be clear on the answers to all of these questions.

4. Knowing your venue

Feeling comfortable in the venue and on the stage is just as important if you are hosting a conference session as if you are speaking at it. You should arrive in good time to have a look at the venue, the stage, the lighting, and the seating. Think about what you have got to do and where you can stand or sit to do it. This will depend on your precise role. You will probably find that the speakers will want some guidance from you as to how you intend to run a question and answer session or debate. They will be nervous and want to know where they should sit, when they should stand up, and so on, just as you would if you were in their position.

5. Know your technology

The technology you need to master may involve some new challenges. Will you have to press any buttons to change slides, especially if you are expected to give out any logistical information? Where are the microphones for you, the speakers, and the audience? Check how many audience microphones there will be and where the people responsible for them will be standing. Have you got a small screen on the desk or the floor in front so that you can see the slides without having to turn your head away from the audience? Always have a hard copy of every presentation, so you can see how far speakers have to go as this will give you a better idea of when you might need to intervene to get a speaker to wrap up.

Before the audience comes in ask the organizers to show you what the lighting will be during the session and the Q&A, as you might be surprised how bright it can be when you are looking out into the auditorium.

Your first job once the event starts is likely to be introducing the session and the speakers.

If you are opening a conference, it is generally best to do so from the main rostrum, introduce the first speaker from there and then return to your seat. Introduce the other speaker(s) from your seat and—as a basic option—host the Q&A from there.

If you are facilitating a session part of the way through the day, introduce it from your chair unless there seems a very good reason for doing otherwise.

Your other option is to do it less formally by using a lapel mic and standing at the front or to one side of the stage. This then leaves the rostrum just for speakers. It is a format that can work, but needs more practice and a presenter that exudes confidence.

At the end of each speech, you should lead the applause, then thank the speaker before going on to introduce the next speaker or the Q&A session.

In addition, do not forget you will usually be the timekeeper for the conference or the session, so make sure you have a watch or clock to hand. The most preferable options for controlling the time people spend at the lectern are some traffic lights, so you can give the speakers warning that they are running out of time, or computer screens with a countdown clock on them. Point these out to the speakers beforehand. If you are using traffic lights, tell them they have got three minutes when the orange light goes on, but give them five. Make it very clear that if the red light goes on, you will intervene if it is not clear that the presentation is drawing to a speedy conclusion.

Dealing with over-running speakers can be hard, but cannot be ducked. You have to make an instant judgment based on several factors: how much further have they got to go (you will only know this if you have their presentation in front of you, which is not always the case), are they boring the audience, or have they got them enthralled, is there any slack in the conference program or are you already running late, has the next speaker got to leave at a specific time?

Do not be afraid to ask someone to wind up if they have over-run, especially if you sense the audience is getting restless: they will thank you. On the other hand, if it is a brilliant speaker who has the audience on the edge of their seats and there is some slack in the conference timetable, let them continue. If someone is doing okay and is just coming to their last couple of slides, similarly let them finish. You need to keep focused on your role as facilitator, not thrust yourself into the audience's conscious-ness as the star of the show or the overbearing controller of all that is going on.

The most difficult part is hosting the question and answer session or a panel debate. You will have to work on developing a range of techniques if you are to be successful. Your objective should always be to bring all of the participants in, as far as possible giving them all equal air time. This is much harder to achieve than it might sound.

The safest option is to stay sitting down with the speaker(s) alongside you, as this keeps you close to them and makes you part of the conversa-tion. If you have a large (four or more) panel of speakers, you could return to the rostrum, although that separates you from them. If you do this, make sure you can see them easily and do not have to turn your back on the audience or the speakers. If you have not got good eye contact with the panelists, you will deny yourself one of the key tools for controlling them, especially if you have to intervene to close someone down if they are dominating the discussion.

A third option is to step onto the front of the stage or down into the area in front of the audience. This will require you to look very confident and assured and is definitely a technique that only experienced chairs should attempt. It can work very well but also it can seem contrived and too showy for some business events.

If you do this, you will need a radio mic and will need to warn the organizers in advance of the event so that they have the right equipment there. It may not be an option if you are expected to take questions through an app or other online system and so need to be able to see a screen. Of course, using a tablet device can be a way around this if you want to move away from a fixed position.

On the whole, stick to what you feel is safest for you, and do not try to be too clever until you have got some experience.

Panel sessions may be made up of people who have already spoken, be standalone sessions with people who need to be introduced or a mixture of the two.

Clearly, if it is a panel made up entirely of people who have already spoken, there is no need to introduce them, perhaps beyond briefly reminding people who they are. If they are people who have not spoken before, then you may choose to ask them to introduce themselves and say a few words about the topic under discussion. This needs to be very carefully managed.

The main point of a panel session is to get a debate going, usually bringing in the audience as soon as possible. Asking panelists to introduce themselves and make a few points about the topic is fraught with danger. All you need is one panelist to decide it is an opportunity to make a speech you are in danger of killing the session. If you have a 45-minute session with four panelists and they all decide to make a short (at least in their minds short) five-minute speech, you have lost almost half of the session before giving the audience any chance to participate. Do not be surprised if they have switched off by the time you turn to them.

If this is the appropriate formula, the participants must be firmly briefed by you beforehand that their opening remarks should be kept to a minimum and focused on stimulating debate and conversation around the panel topic.

There is no magic formula for Q&A and panel sessions. Never assume that because you have good speakers saying something controversial it will run itself with lots of hands going up in the audience or that plenty of questions will be submitted electronically through the event app. Often, at business events, the speakers are very senior and the audience is made up of people junior to them or who might work for them or hope to work for their company one day. These audiences will often be intimidated into silence.

The size of the event can also influence how willing members of the audience will be to ask questions. Generally, the larger the venue and the bigger the audience, the less likely you are to get audience questions. It is at these events that the facility to submit questions electronically (especially if they are allowed to be anonymous) comes into its own.

A part of the art of chairing a panel session is to demonstrate to the audience that the speakers are actually prepared to answer questions, which is why you should always be prepared to ask the first question. Even where there is the option to submit questions electronically, it is often a good idea to have a couple of questions set up in advance to appear on the screen to show the audience it works and that their questions will be put to the panel. It will also give the audience time to log back on and find the right button through which to submit their questions.

If you have to ask some of the questions yourself, you should make the initial question(s) moderately challenging to set the tone for the session. If you can, try to dovetail this with your understanding of the audience's concerns so that you can spin the answer back them and invite responses to it. Always ask the audience for questions first; however, but do not leave a pregnant pause if no hands shoot up. Move on quickly with a phrase such as "While you are thinking of your questions I have got one or two of my own for the panel."

Try to involve all the panelists; although if all the questions from the audience are for one speaker, do not be too contrived in bringing in someone else: this can be a tricky balance to get right. You should stress to the panelists beforehand that you want the session to be engaging and conversational, and that they are welcome to bounce points off each other so that the conversation flows naturally, and you do not have to keep passing the baton from one speaker to the next. Sometimes this works, other times you will have to keep pushing the conversation along.

If you are not getting any take-up from the audience, you will have to make a judgment: is it because they are expecting you to ask all the questions or is it because they are bored, want to go to lunch or go home? Generally, the nearer the end of the day, the less likely they are to join in. If you think they want to pack it up, then do not be afraid to end it early.

However, if an audience likes the way you are asking the questions and feels you have got a good enough grasp of the subject to successfully interrogate the speakers, they may be happy to sit back and leave it to you. It is not necessarily an indication of failure if you cannot generate questions from an audience: it may actually be a complement.

However, when the session finishes, remember to thank the speakers, preferably each one by name and lead a general round of applause for them. Ensure you have their names in front of you at the end of the session. You may think you will know them well enough by then, but the stress of the occasion may make your mind go blank at the crucial moment.

Be wary of thinking you have time to squeeze one more question if the panelists all give you a one word or one sentence answer. You have to be very confident that they will follow your instruction. It can make a fast-paced, impactful end to a panel session, but you have to be certain they are all capable of playing their part. You do not want one panelist taking the opportunity to make all the points they forgot to make earlier in the discussion.

You may have to pass on some organizational information, for instance, where lunch is, what time to be back, or where to go for break-out sessions. Make sure you have all of this clearly noted down on a separate piece of paper, and do not forget it! It is often a good idea to have your wrap up comments and logistical messages on a colored piece of paper so that you can spot it quickly.

The use of interactive technology is becoming more popular, especially when there is a larger audience. This can make for very lively and highly entertaining sessions, but is hard for an inexperienced chair to manage on top of everything else. It is becoming more common, so it is important to get some experience of using it (see Figure 13.1).

Usually, each member of the audience is given a small handset with 10–12 buttons, which they can use to respond to questions, or there might be a conference app or website with everything appearing on their smartphones or tablets.

If you are polling the audience's views on topics, the questions need to be drawn up in advance and put into the system. You may have to use pre-set questions in strict order or you may be able to select questions from those pre-loaded into the system. They usually have multiple choice or simple Yes/No answers. You will need to guide the audience through this process, so familiarity with the system is essential. Some audiences

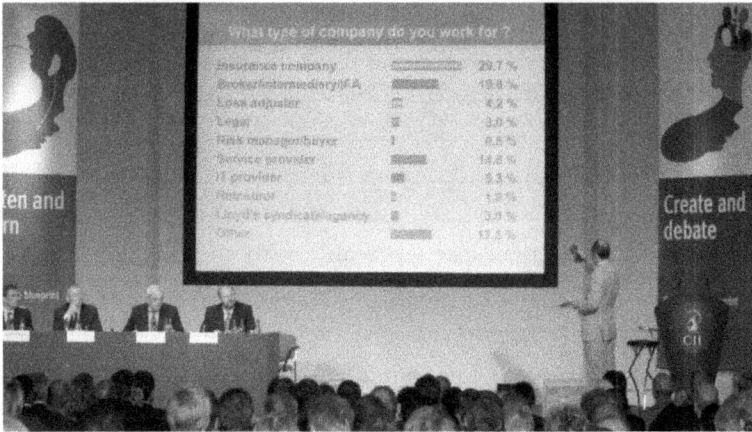

Figure 13.1 Using interactive technology can be very effective, especially at larger events, but requires tight management

Source: Credit: Chartered Insurance Institute

need more encouragement than others, and if they have to log onto a system or download an app, you will need to make sure they have time to do this successfully before asking them to vote. If a presenter tries to rush through the introduction to the system, it often results in embarrassingly low numbers of votes on the early questions, and some members of the audience will give up completely, as they think they have missed the opportunity to participate.

You will also need to cover some of the silence while they are voting so that there are not long periods of silence, which is itself dis-engaging. Once the voting has finished, the answers should appear instantly on the screen. These should be used by you to get reaction from the panel. It sounds easy, but it is not. These sessions only work if you have prepared thoroughly and focus on keeping them moving.

You will need to meet the production team in advance or get them to log you onto the system of their app so that you can see the system they will be using for yourself. Take note of how the handsets work (if they are using them) or how the screens and buttons are laid out. Think about what they say about how questions might be structured and presented and what the options there are for presenting the answers. These may be limited to standard bar graphs and pie charts or may be endless, depending on the system. In the latter case, use only what you think will work with the subject matter and the audience. Do not use a flashy feature simply because it is on offer. Remember that as the results come up on the screen, the audience will expect you to instantly pick out the most interesting aspects of them. If the presentation is too complex, you will find this unnecessarily hard.

Once you have had a run-through and seen how the system works, you will need to draw up or familiarize yourself with a bank of questions to be used during the session. This can be very time consuming, so do not leave it to the last minute. You will need a very clear idea in your own mind as to how the session might run and the sort of issues that will be discussed that can be turned into questions for the audience. If you are hosting a session for an organizer that has already created a list of questions, make sure you feel confident that you understand them, that they are clear with no ambiguities, and that they can be fitted into what you anticipate will be the natural flow of the session. If you do not do this, you will be caught out by the audience member who, on seeing a question they do not think is clear, asks "Can you explain exactly what you mean by X?"

You may also be presented with a system that invites the audience to submit their own questions. This might be through an online system or an app, or it might be in the form of a Twitter feed onto a screen. When these work—with plenty of varied and intelligent questions coming in—they are a great help. When you are faced with a blank screen or irrelevant, poorly formed questions and comments it makes the life of the presenter very hard.

Whichever way it falls, a good panel host will ensure that the online questions are used to enhance the discussion and keep it flowing and will not let them derail it or take it off in a direction the majority of the audience are potentially not interested in.

The best way to make interactive systems work effectively is to engage an audience at the start of a session with a couple of basic demographic questions (for instance, age, sex, job functions). This can often be used to break down the responses afterward—great data for publishers and conference organizers. You might also consider asking a couple of humorous questions before introducing the panel, speakers, and main topics.

This helps people familiarize themselves with the system and to see how the responses are presented.

You will need a short rehearsal on the stage using the technology: insist on this as you need to be confident about where you are going to stand, how easy it is for you to see the screen while maintaining eye contact with both the panel and audience.

Even when you have electronic voting and online questions, discussions still need to be relatively spontaneous, however, and so you will need a bank of questions that cover at least the main options and be prepared to use them flexibly, responding to the flow of the discussion. This can mean preparing more questions than you actually use.

Above all, never forget that every audience is different, and that all audiences are unpredictable. Just because you think the subject is dry, technical, or not especially fresh does not mean an audience will see it that way. Conversely, what seems to you to be a key topic with a well-informed, even controversial, set of panelists may lull you into a false sense of security, thinking that there will be plenty of questions from the audience to fill a session. There may be none. The subject may be one that most members of the audience are frightened to offer an opinion on or they may be intimidated by the reputation or seniority of the speakers.

The lesson is simple: prepare for every eventuality.

Hosting Panel Debates Key Points

- You are in charge, so make sure you know how you are going to run it.
- Timekeeping is important, so be sure you can see a clock or timer and let speakers know how you will manage their time.
- Check names, job titles, and so on, and make sure you know how to pronounce them.
- Thoroughly familiarize yourself with any interactive systems.
- Never make assumptions about how engaged or otherwise an audience will be. You should prepare for every eventuality.

CHAPTER 14

Making Awards Ceremonies Sparkle

This is a big surprise. I don't agree with the concept of award ceremonies, but I'm prepared to make an exception for the ones I'm nominated for. The last time there was a naked man covered in gold paint in my house, it was me.

—Banksy, British graffiti artist

Hosting and presenting awards ceremonies, even modest ones, is one of the toughest presentational roles you can take on.

Awards presentations come in all shapes and sizes, from small lunchtime events to huge evening extravaganzas with spectacular entertainment, lighting, and effects. They all have some things in common, most importantly the reasons why people are there.

Even the most cynical people, such as the graffiti artist Banksy, value the approval of their peers, their industry, or their profession. It is easy to see why individuals, especially those in film, media, and arts, value awards, but industry awards matter too. For a firm to win an award represents valuable third-party endorsement of what they make, supply, how they treat their people, how innovative they are, and so on. The more respected the organization presenting the award, the more valuable that endorsement is.

The people who are there want to win—of course they do—but above all, they want to be treated with respect and made to feel special even if they do not win. These considerations must be at the forefront of a presenter's preparations and presentational style. Shortlists must be made to sound exciting, each finalist made to feel valued, and the winners must feel they have achieved something significant. If the event is dependent for its revenue on sponsorship, the sponsors will want to feel a part of it too.

The other common factor is that awards ceremony audiences are notoriously difficult to engage and frequently get noisy and inattentive, especially if their categories have already been presented and there is plenty of alcohol available. Rowdy does not begin to describe how some awards ceremonies, especially expensive evening events, can get. The host has got to be able to cut-through that.

Hopefully, anyone who is asked to host an awards ceremony for their company or their brand is given plenty of notice and involved at an early stage. This is essential if people want to create a successful event.

There are many different formulas for awards evenings, and they all have their advantages and disadvantages (see Figure 14.1).

Often, awards that have a big budget will bring in a celebrity presenter, and it just becomes a matter of briefing them and writing a script for them that fits the event. However, at some events, the hosting organization likes to have one of its senior people on the stage with the celebrity presenter. This can work well, but brings its own challenges.

The most obvious is the likely mismatch in presentational skills and stage presence between the two. This needs to be addressed in the way the presentations are structured. Who reads the shortlists, who does the link pieces, who announces the winners, and so on. There is no golden

Figure 14.1 Awards ceremonies can be large, glamorous affairs with big budgets such as the British Insurance Awards held in the Royal Albert Hall

Source: Credit: Insurance Post, InfoPro Digital.

rule about what works, as each event is different and the combination of personalities will be unique to that event. It needs careful advance planning, and if you are expected to be on the stage, you should ensure you are involved in that process.

The point at which the audience will be at its most distracted and unsettled will be after an award has been made so, perhaps, that is when an experienced celebrity presenter is best deployed as they will have the best chance of grabbing back their attention and calming them down, if that is necessary.

If you find yourself on the stage with an experienced celebrity, take it as an opportunity to learn from a professional by observing the techniques they use to engage the audience—the way they use their voice, constantly varying pitch and pace, the visual interaction with the audience, and their body language. Despite what will inevitably be your own extreme nerves, try to treat it as a free tutorial.

Second, never try to compete with them. They are the star. Neither they nor the audience want you over-shadowing them. If you try to compete with them, you are very unlikely to win as they will always be able to raise their game to ensure they remain the star. This will be particularly true if humor is part of their act. At worst, you could just embarrass yourself.

You may decide to run the presentation double-handed with a colleague, a formula that often works well as it shares the burden, gives the audiences two voices to listen to and can make the audience easier to control if they know and like the people on the stage.

Whether you are flying solo or working in tandem with someone else, there are some simple techniques that will help you be an effective award ceremony host.

Remember you are going to be on your feet for a long time—many awards presentations last for over an hour—so pace yourself.

You need to establish presence and authority from the start, so a clear, confident opening is essential. You also need to excite people because they have come to an event they expect to be fun and at which they probably plan to enjoy themselves. That is a very positive set of emotions, even if they have a dangerous potential to get out of control. Play to them from the start.

Having established yourself as the person who is going to control the evening, you need to ease back a little. You cannot start in top gear and continue flat out all the way through the event. You will almost certainly have to work hard as the event progresses, to keep the audience engaged and at least reasonably attentive. You need to think of going through the gears in terms of pitch, pace, and projection in order to do this. If you start in top gear and do not change down for a while, you will have little hope of getting an over-excited, noisy audience back and will probably exhaust yourself in the process.

This is never easy, but one solution you should definitely avoid is employing anything that admonishes the audience in terms of what you say or the tone you use. They have come to enjoy themselves, they may have already won an award or be celebrating with friends and clients. They do not want someone on the stage telling them off. Anything that suggests to the audience that you feel you have lost control is rarely effective and can quickly backfire.

It is all about raising your game. This usually means building up the volume and increasing the pace, although you can, if you have a good script, sometimes achieve the desired effect by slowing down, suddenly introducing a greater authority and sense of occasion. Think of going through those gears. Try to judge when you can afford to change down a gear and when you need to change up a few gears very quickly.

The technical crew should play their part in this too by tweaking up your volume as the audience gets louder.

The script should be written to help you with all of this, giving introductions to new categories that say they are important or special in some way and which then imply greater attention is needed. By all means, introduce some categories with a polite request for attention and pause momentarily to see whether it has the desired effect. Such requests have to be made firmly to have any chance of making an impact, but should never come across as losing patience with the audience or telling them off.

Holding a large, excitable audience in a large venue is never easy. You should never convey any sense of feeling you have lost them. If it is noisy and the polite request to pay attention for the next few categories appears not to have worked, then you have to carry on, giving the appearance that you believe it has worked. If you are used to speaking to business audiences that listen in respectful silence, the prospect of speaking while people are talking, laughing, and celebrating can be completely unnerving. You have to look as if you feel you are in control every minute you are on the stage.

A good script will help you.

Often, the first draft of an awards presentation script is done by someone who has never been on the stage and never faced the daunting challenge of keeping an awards presentation alive and engaging. It will contain lists of names, companies, products, schemes, events, or whatever else is being showcased by the awards scheme. Many awards are heavily sponsored, and so their names will be in the script too.

You must review the script thoroughly, always thinking about how each sentence is going to work at the event. Is it a sentence that can be built up to a climax, does it require a slower start before gathering pace, or is it a piece of information that is important but is unlikely to raise a cheer? Announcing sponsors often falls into that latter category. You may feel under pressure to make them feel special, but almost always, the audience is not that interested. The value of an awards sponsorship is delivered on many different levels and the name-check on the day is only part of it. Even if you have to bring someone from the sponsor on the stage to make the presentation, there is no point in giving them a big build-up as the audience will be unlikely to respond. Announce them with sincerity, get them on the stage, and move on. They are a supporting actor, not a star.

If a sponsor is announcing a winner and has to open an envelope Oscars-style to find out who it is, make sure that what is in the envelope is precisely what you want them to say and stress to them that they should not deviate from that. The last thing you need when on the stage hosting an awards event is someone thinking they can start ad libbing alongside you.

You may have to read out lists of finalists. These can vary enormously in length and complexity.

Make sure you master every name. Check any pronunciation that is not immediately obvious and write it out phonetically in your script—even if the script is on an autocue. This should include, where appropriate, an indication of where the stresses should fall in a long, multi-syllabic name. Practice saying out loud all tricky names until you are confident that you will get it right once the adrenalin is pumping around your body on the stage. This is especially important for winners as no one wants their moment of glory spoiled by a host pronouncing their name or the name of their company incorrectly.

Even if you have an autocue, keep your script with you at all times and make sure you put all the pronunciations and any changes in your written script as well as having them shown on the autocue.

At some events, people will want to cheer their colleagues or firms as they are announced on shortlists; at other events, they might just politely applaud; and at some, they might even listen to the shortlists in silence. It is good to have some excitement and build-up to announcing the winners, so if you sense people want to cheer and applaud let them, even encourage it. You have to be sensitive to the audience.

However, if they are a more restrained audience, do not push them to greet the announcements of shortlists and winners in a way they are not going to be comfortable with. If it is an event that has run in the past, ask the organizers how audiences usually respond, so you have a better idea of what to expect.

You should practice the entire script on the stage at a full rehearsal, which should cover all of the sponsor and winner walk-ups, the logistics of handing over trophies, and posing for photographs. If there is going to be music played during the presentations, either live or recorded, then this should be included in the rehearsal. The host needs to feel 100 percent confident they know where they will be standing, where they will have to move to, where sponsors and winners should be standing, and how they are going to move back to the rostrum to continue the presentations.

If there is a live video relay onto screens around a large venue or on big screens behind you, make sure you ask to see how this will look when you are on the stage. It can be quite a shock to suddenly see yourself on a huge screen as you move across the stage. You really do not want any surprises in the middle of such a stressful occasion.

During the rehearsal, make sure you do not over-use your voice. By all means, give everyone a flavor of how you will quicken the pace, up the volume, and boost the projection but do not overdo it. If you feel your voice is straining, take everything back down in terms of volume, make sure you are well hydrated, and try to relax your shoulders, neck, and facial muscles.

Once the rehearsal is out of the way, you need to start thinking about how best to prepare for the big moment on stage. This is where the relaxation techniques discussed in Chapter 3 become very important. No matter how compact, crowded, or chaotic the venue is, try to find somewhere quiet where you can sit down and relax, stretch, and check through your script, especially if you feel there were any passages that did not work, as well as you had hoped during the rehearsal.

If you are expected to give the welcoming speech or be the first person on the stage, then you would be well-advised to avoid the meet-and-greet whirlwind of pre-event receptions. These are far from the ideal preparation for going on the stage. The bigger the event, the more people you will be greeting, but the more daunting the prospect of walking out in front of them a few minutes later will be. You can wait until afterward to talk to everybody: your preparation cannot be done at any other time.

Find somewhere quiet at the back or side of the stage to relax. Check that you have everything you need, review any changes that were made to the script during or after the rehearsal, and make sure they are in both your written script and on the autocue. Make sure you have some water or suitable soft drink, and if you think you might need some further liquid during the presentation, make sure it is on stage and easy to reach. Try to use a glass, rather than a plastic bottle, as it looks much more professional.

The alcohol will usually be flowing at the pre-event receptions, but resist the temptation to drink any. The proverbial *Dutch courage* rarely works well for anyone. You need all your wits about you to manage the complex process of an awards presentation.

Awards Presentation Checklist

- Respect the occasion, respect the winners.
- Understand your role—co-host, sole presenter.
- Authority and a good stage presence is vital.
- Learn to *go through the gears*, building up momentum and excitement, but also know when to slow down, perhaps to add authority.
- You must remain in control, but never admonish the audience for being noisy.
- A good script is essential, and you need to own it.
- Check all names and pronunciations.
- Rehearse thoroughly.
- Make time to relax before going on the stage.

CHAPTER 15

Social Events: A Different Challenge

Be sincere; be brief; be seated.
> —Franklin D. Roosevelt, American President

This book is primarily about conference speeches and business presentations, but once you get a reputation as a competent speaker, you will inevitably be asked to speak at many other occasions. These will range from staff leaving parties, industry or association dinners, family occasions, and even funerals.

At the top of the list of social occasions to fear for many people are the speeches made at weddings. Almost everyone will be able to recall a wedding where they have sat through one or more excruciatingly awful speeches. There is really little excuse for this. At the very least, following Franklin D Roosevelt's advice should get most people through most speeches at weddings and social occasions with minimal mishap, with their dignity intact, and hopefully, with guests who feel the speaker has done a competent job (see Figure 15.1).

As ever, the key to being successful is preparation. What is your role? How many people will be there? When do I speak? Where do I speak from? How long should I speak for?

At most weddings, there are set roles for each speaker to perform in terms of proposing toasts and focusing on particular members of the wedding party, but modern weddings often vary these, so make sure that, if you are asked to speak at a wedding, you know exactly what tasks you are expected to carry out as part of your speech.

Formal weddings share many of the characteristics of formal dinners where various people are expected to speak at the end, some willingly, others less so.

Figure 15.1 *Weddings and other formal social occasions can be*
very daunting but with proper preparation they can be tackled with
confidence and success. The author's wife, Mariette Mason, speaking
at their daughter's wedding

Pic credit: John Burgess

After-dinner speaking is an art in itself with plenty of pitfalls, such as inebriated audiences or having to follow either the most appalling speaker in the world or the most entertaining outside of the West End: dinners seem to attract the extremes.

The toughest speech is the one that is expected to be funny. This may be the final speaker at a dinner or the Best Man at a wedding. Unless you are a natural comedian, these are among the most daunting public speaking roles. They are very hard to get right, but very easy to get horribly wrong.

There are whole books on after-dinner speaking and Best Man's speeches, which are full of useful advice on these very specialist areas, usually including a lot of jokes that can be adapted for different situations. If you think your career will take you down this route, then you should start collecting jokes that you might be able to use or adapt. It is always best to have some original material, but it will need to be carefully crafted and tried out on other people first.

This advice about testing out jokes on colleagues, friends, and relatives who will give you an honest opinion applies even more on these occasions, especially after-dinner speaking. Never fall into the trap of creating a routine that works well for one audience and automatically think it will work well for all audiences.

The make-up of the audiences might be very different; there may be subjects that were fine to treat humorously for one audience or group of people that are completely off-limits for others. You may even have more than one audience in the same room at the same time and so need to be sensitive across a range of topics and also include material of interest to each sub-audience.

One of the most common mistakes at weddings is that people address speeches and jokes to one section of what is usually a very diverse audience. Risky humor that might appeal to the generation of the bride and groom might be deeply offensive to members of the older generations or other branches of the family who are also present. Think very hard about the audience and pitch it so that you have something that will appeal to everyone, without offending anyone else.

Often, well-told stories work well on social occasions, whether they are weddings, leaving speeches, and even funeral eulogies. They are usually occasions when the focus is on one or more individuals, so building a strong narrative around them engages friends, colleagues, and relatives. The structure of the speech should be simple and logical. You should work hard on the opening so that you set the tone for the whole speech, remembering that you may want to blend humor, personal stories, some serious points, and specific tasks into one speech.

Telling stories and jokes requires careful preparation. They need to be well structured and well told. With jokes in particular, timing is often crucial, so practice them both privately and with friends and colleagues so that you can be confident that you will make the best use of such material.

Think about how you are going to vary the tone and pace as your speech progresses. This is even more important at social events, as audiences will be more relaxed, but also, potentially, more easily distracted. It is quite often the case that audiences are almost as apprehensive about the speeches as the speaker(s). This is both a challenge and an opportunity.

It is a challenge because you have to ensure you get them with you right from the start; otherwise, they might make a snap judgment that you are about to fulfill their worst fears about what to expect.

The opportunity you have is that, by establishing the right tone and quality from the start, you will have their attention and will have created a sense of expectation that you will be worth listening to.

Of course, audiences at social events are there to do much more than listen to speeches. This means they might be restless, noisy, and even disruptive (we will look at how to deal with disruptions in Chapter 16). You have to be prepared to work through this, using pitch, pace, and pauses to good effect. Be sensitive to how your audience is responding to your content: are they applauding where you expected them to, are they laughing, how long are they laughing for, are the responding in an unexpected way? As hard as it might seem, you need to learn to listen to the audience and ride their emotions. Work with them, not against them.

The type of venue, its layout, and the quality of sound systems (if available) vary enormously when it comes to informal speaking situations and social occasions. You will often find yourself having to cope with a less than ideal setup—certainly one that is far removed from the professional stages and well-managed technical backup at most formal business events.

Try to put yourself in control as far as possible. Check out the arrangements as best you can before the bulk of the audience arrive. Go through your established checklist of when you are expected to speak, how or if you will be introduced, do you have to walk far to where you will be speaking from, negotiate steps, what sort of microphone will be available, will you have a lectern for your notes or script? If you are unhappy with the arrangements, see if you can get the most serious shortcomings rectified. This is not always possible at a social event, so do not let anything that is less than perfect unduly distract or upset you.

Often, the biggest challenges will be the venue and layout. Social occasions and wedding receptions in hotels often present very tricky configurations in terms of the shape of the room and arrangement of tables. Rooms can be long and thin, with people a long way to either side of you, there might be pillars, large flower arrangements, or people seated with their backs to where you are expected to speak from. Generally, these are the things that you can do very little about. Note them and think about how you can overcome them to the best of your ability using all the techniques we have discussed in earlier chapters.

What you may be able to get something done about is lighting, the provision of a lectern if you prefer to use one, and the microphones.

If you are using notes or a script, you will need decent lighting. You would think that most venues used for hosting social events would realize that speakers should be well-lit so that the audience's eyes are drawn toward them and so speakers can see their notes, but this is not always the case. Ask to see the lighting and see if it can be adjusted if you are not happy with it.

Almost all venues familiar with social events that include speeches will have lecterns, either small ones that can be placed on the table in front of a speaker or free-standing ones placed to one side that the speakers move to when they speak. If you prefer to use a lectern and one is not immediately in evidence, ask for it to be provided. If you have visualized yourself speaking with your notes or script resting in front of you so that you can use a variety of gestures, you will probably find it quite awkward and unnerving to have to manage without one.

The quality of microphones and sound systems in hotels and similar venues varies enormously. It should go without saying that you should, if at all possible, try it out before you speak. Check you know whether you have to turn it on, and if so, precisely how you do that. That last thing any speaker should do at the beginning of their speech is ask the audience if the microphone is working or whether they can be heard.

A special category of speech is the eulogy at a funeral or memorial occasion. It goes without saying that these need to be crafted with great sensitivity. There may be things about the deceased that are best left unsaid in public, so make sure you know where these boundaries are. The best eulogies are usually a blend of seriousness, appropriate solemnity, and lighter touches, even humorous at time. This is not easy to achieve. The best advice is to focus on telling a story about the person, their life and achievements. If you do this, then the all-important ingredient—sincerity—is most likely to shine through.

They can be very emotional occasions, especially the funeral itself. You should be prepared for an emotional response from family and friends—and from yourself. You may find it hard to carry on: pause, look out to the back of the church or hall, take a deep breath, even close your eyes if that helps, and try to return to the script at the beginning of a sentence or paragraph. Do not apologize: nobody will think badly of you.

The venues for such events vary enormously from huge churches to more intimate settings. One advantage they usually have is that they are designed around people speaking to congregations, so where you speak from, microphones, and so on are usually pretty much built into the venue. Of course, religious buildings are all very different, so it is a good idea to arrive early, walk around, and get a feel for the place and where you will be speaking from.

As you can see, the range of occasions you can be asked to speak at is very wide once you get a reputation for being good on your feet. The better a speaker people believe you are, the more you will be asked to provide a few appropriate words at all sorts of events. Take it as a compliment. Most of the people asking know that they could not perform the role as well as you.

Speeches for Social Occasions

- Make sure you know precisely what you role is and what is expected of you.
- Be careful with humor: keep it appropriate and make sure you use it well.
- Practice your speech, especially the humor.
- Check out the venue.
- Listen to the audience and work with their emotional responses.

CHAPTER 16

How to Improve

All great speakers were bad speakers first.
—Ralph Waldo Emerson, American author and poet

Experience is obviously the best way to improve. There is no substitute for getting out there in front of an audience and giving it a go. However, do not fall into the trap of thinking you have mastered the art of public speaking and have nothing more to learn just because you have had a few presentations that have gone well. There is plenty that can trip you up, no matter how experienced you are, and there will always be something you can improve on.

If you really want to become a first-class speaker, aim for incremental improvement. This is an intensely practical skill, and you will only improve and progress through experience. This means being confident enough to accept opportunities to speak when they come along: put aside your anxieties and seize those opportunities.

Early in your public speaking career, there will be opportunities that you genuinely feel are beyond your capabilities, so be careful not to set yourself up to fail. If something comes along that you really do not feel you are ready for, set it as an objective to build your confidence and expand your speaker's toolkit sufficiently that one day—not too far away—you will be able to tackle it.

Small-scale presentations, especially if they are relatively low key or among trusted colleagues, are often a good opportunity to try out a new technique or two. Perhaps, a new style of introduction, a rhetorical ending, or more ambitious variations in pitch and pace could be trialed without fearing too severe a consequence, should it not quite come off. See if you can make something you have not tried before work for you.

If you get the opportunity to make the same speech several times—perhaps a series of repeated presentations to different departments, a customer roadshow, sales presentation, or a fundraising appeal—take it. Being able to work with the same material is one of the best methods of polishing up your style and reflecting on whether the structure of your presentation is communicating your message(s) to maximum effect.

If it is a sales presentation, perhaps the passages creating a sense of need lose their way a little or the call to action—the sales pitch—is not clear or direct enough. Often, business sales pitches fail early on because they try to tell people too much about their own business. Every time you make a presentation, you should evaluate how effective it was and improve it appropriately.

It could be stylistic facets that need improving. Did you have enough variation in pitch and pace, or were you too timid in the way you used your voice? Could you have used the slides more effectively, or did you make the mistake of spending too much time talking to the screen and not to the audience?

If you sit back and genuinely congratulate yourself on a presentation that was successful, ask yourself what could I have done better? How could I take it to another level?

Listen to advice, observe others, and be constructive in your self-appraisal. If you want to improve in any form of public speaking, listening to the views of others is very important—prompt them for their views if necessary.

After each presentation, sit down and reflect on what worked and what could be improved. Perhaps, it is a turn of phrase, or sentences, that contains too many ideas and does not help the audience focus on your core message. May be the narrative does not flow as well as you hoped because it moves too abruptly from one topic to the next without creating a sense of anticipation or expectation first. If possible, involve friends and colleagues in reviewing your performance, especially if they can be trusted to give honest, but constructive opinions.

This should not necessarily just be people who you respect as good performers. You should also ask people who make up the audiences you speak to whether it was what they expected, whether they enjoyed it, and how it came across. After all, audiences are rather important at live events. Some of their comments may be useful, some may not: you must learn to sift through such advice.

If you have spoken at an event where structured audience feedback has been collected, have the courage to ask for it and look at how you rated against the others speakers at the event. If there are speakers who secured higher audience ratings than you, try to reflect on why. Was there anything they did that helped them engage the audience that you could have done?

Watch other speakers and presenters, and observe the techniques they use. They may have particularly effective ways of introducing people, of linking different topics, introducing appropriate humor, or explaining complex subjects with great clarity. Their presentation might make good use of lists, both in terms of the way it is written and the way they deliver them. The way they use their eyes to engage with the audience and incorporate gestures to bring key points alive might be particularly effective.

The list is endless. But, the key is to watch and learn.

Many of the great speeches of the last 100 years can be watched or listened to online. Of course, they will be among the very best speeches ever made given by people who were totally in command of their audience and supremely confident in themselves. That does not mean you cannot learn from them. In particular, look for those variations of pitch and pace, the use of pauses, and the overall construction of their narrative.

You may see an experienced professional speaker deliver an amazing presentation and think "I could never do that." However, there will almost certainly be some aspect of their style, some little trick, or polished technique that you could take, add to your toolkit and try one day. If you do not keep trying to improve and develop your style, you will not merely stop progressing, but you will stagnate, become predictable, and ultimately, dull.

No matter how many presentations and speeches you have given, never make the mistake of believing you have nothing to learn.

There are many courses, one-to-one coaching schemes that benefit experienced speakers as well as beginners. Going on a course will expose you to new ideas, force you out of your comfort zone, and give you a chance to share with other people some of your experiences, fears, and hopes. It will give you a first-hand insight into what works, and just as important, what does not work.

As well as learning to seek and listen to the views of others, you must learn to honestly appraise yourself.

There is no point in practicing a speech if you are not going to be self-critical and determined to improve, but remember, do not analyze your performance to the point of self-destruction. If something is not working, then think about how you can improve it. If you can put it right before taking to the stage, fine, but if it has not worked as well as you wanted during a speech, try to work out why and think about how to improve it for next time.

You can learn from failure too. If you set out to achieve a particular objective and clearly did not succeed in achieving it, have the courage to ask yourself and others why not.

Failure, partial or otherwise, might not always be down to you. Speeches are live events, and live events can go wrong.

There are so many things outside your control that you might think it is almost hardly worth worrying about, or you might worry about them far too much. The more preparation you do, the easier you are likely to find it to cope with anything unexpected.

Some of the problems you might encounter and which could destroy all that excellent work you have done to get your nerves under control include the following.

Off-Stage Noises

These could be sudden, such as plates being dropped, or continuous noise, such as drilling or an alarm going off.

If it is a sudden, one off noise, pause and compose yourself. Continue, perhaps, making a witty remark about someone who might be expected to disagree with what you are saying or you did not expect to have quite such a dramatic impact. You may have to recap a few sentences if the noise cut across a particularly complex passage or a story with a strong narrative.

If the noise is continuous, you have to make a decision about whether it is worth soldiering on. If it is very loud, you might want to suggest a short break while the organizers sort it out. Look to the conference chair or event host for advice. If they are any good, they will quickly form a judgment about whether the noise makes it impossible for the audience to listen to the presentation.

Microphone Failure

This can take two forms: interference such as buzzing or a constant whine, or total failure.

Sometimes, it might cause be some sudden feedback if you are walking around with a hand-held or lapel mic and cross over with the signal from another microphone. This is something you must learn to check during rehearsals.

With interference in a sound system, again it is a matter of judgment—mainly yours—as to whether it is a major problem. You can always pause and ask the audience whether they find it so bad that it makes it impossible to listen to you. The sound engineers might appreciate this as it will give them an opportunity to try a quick fix with a replacement microphone or adjustment of the sound levels on the control desk.

When it comes to a sound system or microphone failure, it is down to you and your voice against the venue. If you are confident you can project your voice to the back of the room, then keep going. If you cannot, then, if at all possible, wait until the problem is fixed.

Interruptions and Hecklers

It is extremely rare for business speakers to be interrupted or heckled by members of the audience. That sort of treatment is usually reserved for politicians, but it might happen. If it does, the most important thing is to stay calm.

You could be delivering bad news to a group of employees, some of whom might be very upset by it because of the impact it has on them. You may be talking about a controversial topic at a business event that has attracted some dissenters with strong feelings on the topic. It might be an inebriated audience at a social event, who think they are funny by interrupting you.

There are no easy ways or simple formulas for dealing with interruptions. The last resort should be taking them on, attacking them or alienating them, as this will usually provoke them further unless it is done perfectly, and that means getting exactly the right words and delivering them in exactly the right way. There are a few techniques to try before launching into a full-frontal battle with the perpetrators, however.

If it happens, it is best initially to pause and look in their direction. If they have made people laugh, then acknowledge that with a smile and quickly pick up the thread of your speech. If they have not made anyone engage with them through humor, then make sure your look is disapproving in the best traditions of the fiercest of school teachers.

You can escalate your response very gradually, depending on the circumstances. Sometimes, just repeating the point that has antagonized them, but more forcefully is enough to see them off. You could preface this with a firm indication that you will not be put off, "Let me repeat…," "I say again …," or similar. Obviously, this needs to be done in a firm tone clearly indicating that you have not been intimidated.

Sometimes, people interrupt because they feel their point of view is being deliberately overlooked and will not get an airing. Perhaps, reassuring them that they can have their say at the end if the structure of the event allows for that would help calm them down. If you can couch this as an appeal to give you a fair hearing, you will be more likely to win the audience's sympathy.

Firm hand gestures can help too, indicating they should stop or quieten down. These should always be used in a way that shows you are still in control. Although it does depend on the nature of the interruption, usually any suggestion of weakness or feeling that you have been put off by them will only encourage them.

This is why you have to be very careful about taking them on. It can suggest to them that they have wrested control from you. It might inflame them further, in which case, regaining control will become very, very difficult, and you risk losing your dignity along the way. If you are aware of the reasons why they have interrupted and have mentally gone through how to respond, you might have a well-honed phrase ready. This should really be trying to do one or two things (or both if you are really clever).

The first is be as brutally but politely dismissive of their point as you can. The second is to get the rest of the audience on your side. If you are dealing with inebriated guests at a social event, the best bet is to keep the second objective firmly in your sights, as you will probably only incite the drunks further and earn their loudly expressed derision if you try to dismiss or belittle them.

Just be aware that these things can happen. Do not fret about them. They are outside your control, and nobody will blame you for them.

Improving Checklist

- Learn from others.
- Take a step at a time, but constantly try to improve.
- Look for opportunities to speak and try new techniques in terms of content and delivery.
- Seek feedback and listen to others.
- Never stop learning.

Dealing with Problems

- Stay calm.
- Can you do anything about it?
- Think of the audience and how you can get them on your side.
- Start with firm, low-key responses that maintain your control and dignity.
- Be very wary about taking on hecklers unless you are confident of victory.

Conclusion

It is ridiculous that so many people inhibit their career development by shying away from opportunities to shine in front of others, whether they be colleagues, clients, or peers. It is almost impossible to progress in any walk of life if you are not prepared to make that journey from behind your desk to the front of the stage.

You may never come to enjoy it. Some people love performing and relish the opportunity to get to their feet. Most people do not fall into that category, but they can still grow to become very competent, confident speakers.

Hopefully, the advice in this book will help many more people do just that.

Finally. Good luck!

About the Author

David Worsfold *is best known for his work as an award-winning financial journalist, in particular as a writer on the insurance industry and financial services which he has covered for over 35 years.*

As well as editing a range of leading business titles, David wrote for *The Guardian* for several years and has contributed to most major national newspapers in the UK. He has appeared on radio and television as a commentator on insurance and financial issues and is an experienced conference speaker and facilitator.

He has created an innovative range of training courses and coaching modules for people who need to move from behind their desk to the front of the stage as part of their job. These have been run successfully for over 20 years, helping hundreds of people to be more confident and effective presenters.

Among his many achievements, David launched the British Insurance Awards—now the most successful B2B awards scheme in the UK and in 1990 he established the All Party Parliamentary Group on Insurance & Financial Services which has played an influential role in improving communication between the insurance and retail financial services sectors and Parliament.

His first book, *Fighting for the Empire*, a military biography, was published by Sabrestorm in September 2016. A second military history book on Operation Aerial—the evacuations from France in June 1940 after the fall of Dunkirk—is planned for publication in early 2020.

He has also written *Twitter for Financial Services*, published by Business Expert Press in December 2017.

Index

OTHER TITLES IN THE HUMAN RESOURCE MANAGEMENT AND ORGANIZATIONAL BEHAVIOR COLLECTION

- *Conflict and Leadership: How to Harness the Power of Conflict to Create Better Leaders and Build Thriving Teams* by Christian Muntean
- *Creating the Accountability Culture: The Science of Life Changing Leadership* by Yvonnne Thompson
- *Managing Organizational Change: The Measurable Benefits of Applied iOCM* by Linda C. Mattingly
- *Lead Self First Before Leading Others: A Life Planning Resource* by Stephen K. Hacker and Marvin Washington
- *The HOW of Leadership: Inspire People to Achieve Extraordinary Results* by Maxwell Ubah
- *Leading the High-Performing Company: A Transformational Guide to Growing Your Business and Outperforming Your Competition* by Heidi Pozzo
- *The Concise Coaching Handbook: How to Coach Yourself and Others to Get Business Results* by Elizabeth Dickinson
- *How Successful Engineers Become Great Business Leaders* by Paul Rulkens
- *Redefining Competency Based Education: Competence for Life* by Nina Jones Morel and Bruce Griffiths

Announcing the Business Expert Press Digital Library

Concise e-books business students need for classroom and research

This book can also be purchased in an e-book collection by your library as

- a one-time purchase,
- that is owned forever,
- allows for simultaneous readers,
- has no restrictions on printing, and
- can be downloaded as PDFs from within the library community.

Our digital library collections are a great solution to beat the rising cost of textbooks. E-books can be loaded into their course management systems or onto students' e-book readers.
The **Business Expert Press** digital libraries are very affordable, with no obligation to buy in future years. For more information, please visit **www.businessexpertpress.com/librarians**. To set up a trial in the United States, please email **sales@businessexpertpress.com**.

www.ingramcontent.com/pod-product-compliance
Lightning Source LLC
Chambersburg PA
CBHW071909200326
41519CB00016B/4547